rhetoric

The Ancient Art of Public Discourse for the 21st Century Speaker

Crystal L. Etzel, Ph.D.

FOURTH EDITION

Kendall Hunt publishing company

Cover images © Shutterstock.com

Kendall Hunt
publishing company

www.kendallhunt.com
Send all inquiries to:
4050 Westmark Drive
Dubuque, IA 52004-1840

Copyright © 2014, 2015, 2017, 2020 by Crystal L. Etzel

ISBN 978-1-7924-0968-4

Kendall Hunt Publishing Company has the exclusive rights to reproduce this work,
to prepare derivative works from this work, to publicly distribute this work,
to publicly perform this work and to publicly display this work.

All rights reserved. No part of this publication may be reproduced,
stored in a retrieval system, or transmitted, in any form or by any
means, electronic, mechanical, photocopying, recording, or otherwise,
without the prior written permission of the copyright owner.

Printed in the United States of America

Contents

Introduction: What Are We Doing Here? v

Part One—Aristotle and Aphthonius and Cicero, Oh My! 1

Chapter 1	Some Early History of Public Speaking and Why You Should Know About It 3
Chapter 2	Beginning with Aristotle 13
Chapter 3	Roll Out the Canons 23
Chapter 4	Let's Argue 33
Chapter 5	Let's Argue Some More 43
Chapter 6	Let's NOT Argue Like This 51

Part Two—The Progymnasmata 61

Chapter 7	Exercise 1—Fable 63
Chapter 8	Exercise 2—Tale or Narrative 71
Chapter 9	Exercise 3—Chreia 77
Chapter 10	Exercise 4—Proverb 83
Chapter 11	Exercises 5 and 6—Refutation/Confirmation 87
Chapter 12	Exercise 7—Commonplace 95
Chapter 13	The Ceremonial Speech Exercises 8 and 9—Encomium/Invective 99
Chapter 14	The Informative Speeches Exercises 10, 11, 12—Comparison, Descriptive, Characterization 105
Chapter 15	The Persuasive Speech—The Deliberative and Forensic Exercises Exercises 13 and 14—Thesis and the Introduction to Law 117

Appendices 137

| Appendix 1 | Self-Analysis .... 137 |
| Appendix 2 | Speech Critiques .... 167 |

Bibliography 195

Introduction

WHAT ARE WE DOING HERE?

How does one become a competent public speaker? Public Speaking teachers have been asking this question for a very long time. There are many answers to this question. The answer this book chooses is The Progymnasmata.

The Progymnasmata is close to 2,500 years old. The ancient Greeks and later the ancient Romans used it to teach their students the fundamentals of good public speaking. The Progymnasmata is a group of fourteen or so basic exercises that when artfully constructed allow a speaker to produce the *gymnasmatum*—a full-blown public address. Public Speaking was important to the workings of both the Greek city state and the Roman Republic. The Greek or Roman citizen had a responsibility to be competent in public speaking because in a direct democracy like Greece or a republic like Rome, the citizen might be called on at any time to speak in the Greek agora or before the Roman senate.

The ancient teachers taught their students the **art (techne)** of public address. They taught them through small exercises in oratory and argument so that they could give their students the building blocks of a speech and asked them to put those blocks in whatever order they thought necessary to produce a well-crafted, interesting, persuasive, and unique speech.

The purpose of this text is to teach you how to craft your speeches the way the ancient Greeks and Romans did theirs; the way Medieval and Renaissance Europeans did theirs; the way modern Americans do theirs; by studying public speaking the old-fashioned way, you will be on the road to learn the Art of Rhetoric.

PART ONE
Aristotle and Aphthonius and Cicero, Oh My!

© Anastasios71/Shutterstock.com

Since this textbook contains a very old way of learning how to speak in public we should begin at the beginning. This section of the text will introduce you to the following:

- ✔ A short discussion of where the original exercises come from
- ✔ Who the big players were
- ✔ What the big players wrote and said about public speaking
- ✔ The basics of public speaking
- ✔ How to argue
- ✔ How not to argue

Some of this material is practical knowledge you will use when you compose and deliver your speech. Things like:

- ✔ Organization
- ✔ Use of voice
- ✔ Visual Aids
- ✔ Appearance

Other ways of thinking

✔ What makes a good argument
✔ How do you avoid persuasive fallacies
✔ How to do audience analysis and how to use the findings

© marekuliasz/Shutterstock.com

By the time you finish a speech class which uses the Progymnasmata it is possible you will have heard over 200 speeches. You personally will have delivered as many as 14 of those. From Fable to Introduction to Law you will have been exposed to a great deal of information, persuasion, and praise or censure of people, places, and things. As a result:

❏ You will know what makes a good argument and what does not.
❏ You will be able to make fact, values, or policy arguments.
❏ You will be able to tell stories with emotion and meaning.
❏ You will be able to uphold virtue.
❏ You will be able to denounce vice.
❏ You will be able to praise the praiseworthy.
❏ You will be able to condemn the condemnable.

The Progymnasmata has a long and storied history of helping orators produce memorable speeches. You are now part of that history. You are like the great speakers of old and the great speakers of today. You have here in this text all you need to become an accomplished speaker. You will no longer have to worry about whether you have anything to say. Grab your Progymnasmata and pull out a tale, a proverb, a confirmation, and refutation and get going.

If you have to give a toast, a business presentation, or a campaign speech you now have the tools to make that campaign speech, business presentation, or toast into something memorable.

So here we go.

CHAPTER 1

Some Early History of Public Speaking and Why You Should Know About It

© ibreakstock/Shutterstock.com

Let's start by taking a look at the history of Public Speaking. Why should we do that? Well, because it's interesting. Plus it will tell us things we can use when constructing speech in twenty-first century America. That last statement might not seem obvious, but it is true.

Everything you learn about public speaking in any college in America today was taught to young scholars in ancient Greece, in ancient Rome, in Dark Ages monasteries, in Medieval universities, in European form schools, and in American one-room schoolhouses.

We fell away from this ancient method of teaching the art of rhetoric or, if you prefer, the art of public speaking, in the last century. This text aims to revive the old method. Why? Well, it did produce some *very* good speakers.

Our discussion will use the terms rhetoric and public speaking interchangeably so don't get confused.

We will start our discussion using Socrates's method for educating his students and ask some questions.

What Is Rhetoric?

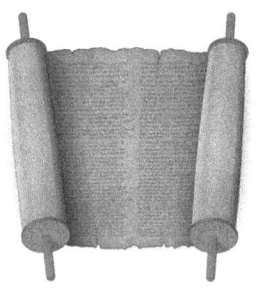
© GI/Shutterstock.com

According to Aristotle, rhetoric is the art of finding all of the available means of persuasion in the given case.

The Greek word translated as "art" that Aristotle uses here is "techne" the title of our textbook. Techne means craft, craftsmanship, a practical skill, and of course, art in Greek. See how easily the idea of learning the art of public speaking fits into the idea of rhetoric being a craft or practical skill?

Notice that Aristotle believes that **ALL** rhetoric is inherently persuasive. And he is right to think so. Even when giving an informative speech the speaker is attempting to persuade the audience that the information given is correct and should be believed. The underlying principle in this textbook is that all public address is persuasive even if all you are doing is explaining to a class how to wire a lamp.

How did the first rhetoricians view rhetoric?

- The ancients saw rhetoric as a tool used to influence politics and policy.
- The ancients viewed the study of rhetoric as equivalent to the study of citizenship.
    - Your success and influence as a citizen and a man (sorry ladies, only men could be citizens in ancient Athens) depended on your ability to speak well.
- The ancients expected disagreement because of how they viewed the world.

How did the ancient rhetoricians use rhetoric?

- To make decisions.
- Resolve disputes.
- Mediate discussion of important topics.
- Choose the best course of action when there was disagreement.

What kind of questions did the old rhetoricians ask that helped them develop and deliver speeches?

- How do I best go about writing a speech?
- Is there a process I can use to do this and if so what is it?
- What should be in a speech?
- Should a speech be organized and if so how?
- Does it matter what words I use?
- Does it matter how I deliver my speech?
- Can good delivery be taught?

Should we be asking the same questions? Why, yes we should. Nothing has changed in the last 2,500 years that would have fundamentally changed the way we engage in persuasion. Those seven questions are as important now as they were when they were first asked.

The next important question is:

Where do we start in our study of rhetoric and speechmaking?

- Most scholars trace the origins of Western rhetoric to the Greeks and Romans.
- They do this because of the nature of the political and social culture of these civilizations.
- And it is true that the Greek and Roman cultures have influenced Western culture a great deal. Both influenced
  - Music
  - Art
  - Literature
  - Language

It is not surprising then that these two cultures would influence how rhetoric was taught and the type of rhetoric Western culture eventually adopted.

Why Greece?

- Greece had a well-established democracy.
- Citizens were expected to be able to speak persuasively in the agora (the public square), in the courts, and in ceremonial situations.
- This expectation gave rise to the teaching of effective public speaking.

Why Rome?

© Vythoulkas/Shutterstock.com

- Greece begins to decline. Rome filled the void.
- Rome comes to dominate the world. It is not surprising that her rhetoricians become famous and popular.
- Rome had a senate and it was important for senators to be able to speak persuasively.

There were many practitioners of the art of public speaking in the ancient world. So who are the important people to know? Try these:

© Gariepy/Shutterstock.com

Corax and Tisias (Sicily)

Circa 467 BCE

Corax was one of the first teachers of rhetoric.

Corax believed that even if a speaker had a weak case a good speech would allow the speaker to prevail over an opponent.

The first to divide speeches into:

- Introduction
- Narration
- Confirmation
- Confutation
- Peroration

© tsaplia/Shutterstock.com

Isocrates (Greek)

436–338 BCE

Contemporary of Plato

Had a school of rhetoric in Athens.

He believed that rhetoric could be used and studied to help ordinary people with everyday problems.

© gdvcom/Shutterstock.com

The Sophists (Greek)

Fifth Century BCE

These were traveling teachers who charged tuition.

Taught the following:

- ❏ Style and delivery could overcome a weak case.
- ❏ Public opinion important.
- ❏ Style over substance was fine if it enhanced your case.

Source: Public Domain

Plato (Greek)

427–347 BCE

He believed the sophists were unethical.

The end of rhetoric is truth-seeking.

Substance and truth matter.

© Anastasios71/Shutterstock.com

Aristotle (Greek)

394–322 BCE

When people think about rhetoric they think about Aristotle.

He was a pupil of Plato.

Wrote *The Art of Rhetoric.*

Gave the definition of rhetoric we will use in class: **Rhetoric is the art of finding all of the available means of persuasion in the given case.**

Defined the three most important general proofs to be used for persuasive purposes:

- **Ethos**—appeal to character
- **Pathos**—appeal to emotion
- **Logos**—appeal to reason

© Karas/Shutterstock.com

Provided three general categories of discourse:

- **Forensic**—legal oratory
- **Deliberative**—political
- **Epideictic**—ceremonial

He began to construct a theory of style. This is where the ethical use of style and delivery starts.

Aristotle was more concerned with content than delivery.

Demosthenes (Greek)

384–322 BCE

He was a contemporary of Aristotle.

He is believed to be the greatest of the Greek orators.

He is said to have filled his mouth with pebbles and shouted at the sea to strengthen his voice.

And he made his living by defending wealthy clients in court.

Source: Project Gutenburg

Hermagoras of Temnos (Greek)

Mid-second century BCE

© dedMazay/Shutterstock.com

Opposed by Cicero. Defended by Quintilian.

Thought to have developed Stasis Theory.

Inventor of what has become known as the five W's.

(Although he had a division of seven) who, what, when, where, why, in what way, by what means.

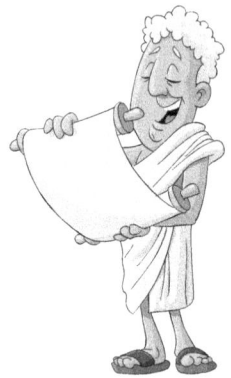

Cicero (Roman)

90 BCE

© Renata Sedmakova/Shutterstock.com

Improved on **Stasis Theory**

- ❑ In Greek stasis means "strife" and "immobility." In rhetoric stasis means: the place or ground of the dispute.
- ❑ All arguments or controversies are based on the grounds of the dispute. Everyone has to be on the same page or you can't have a decent argument.

So there are questions that need to be asked in order for a good argument to be made.

- ❑ **Fact:** Does the thing exist? (Is there a crisis in Social Security?)
- ❑ **Value:** What is the nature of the thing? (Is Social Security good or bad?)
- ❑ **Policy:** What should be done? (Should we privatize Social Security?)

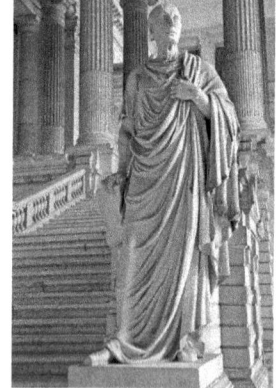

Cicero used Aristotle's rhetorical appeals to fill in the classical pattern of organization.

- ❑ In the **exordium or introduction,** you should establish your credibility so a speaker should use **ethos appeals** here.
- ❑ In the **narration, confirmation, and refutation** part of the speech the speaker should use logos appeals.
- ❑ In the **conclusion,** go for the **pathos** appeals.

He is considered to be the greatest practioner of ancient rhetoric and its greatest theorist.

Quintilian (Roman)

Circa 35–100 CE

Is known for his definition of rhetoric: "A good man speaking well."

Wrote an important compilation of ancient rhetoric.

Thought to be the greatest teacher of rhetoric ever.

The above list tells you what about the birth of public speaking as a discipline?

- ❏ That speaking well is an important aspect of an educated person's life
- ❏ That there is a method by which one can design and deliver an effective public address
- ❏ That there are three basic types of appeals to audience
- ❏ Audience is important

Synthesis Questions

- ❏ What is important to note about these teachers of rhetoric?
  - ▪ Rhetoric is persuasive.
  - ▪ Good arguments well-delivered can overcome a weak case.
  - ▪ The citizen is required to be versed in the means of persuasion.
  - ▪ Public speaking is an art/practical skill.
  - ▪ The art/practical skill can be taught.
- ❏ Do you agree with Quintilian's definition?
- ❏ What does Aristotle mean by art?

The Greeks and Romans wrote books about rhetoric. There were a lot of them. We use them today as the basis for the textbooks produced for public speaking classes. What are the texts we need to know and why do we need to know them?

Aristotle

The Art of Rhetoric

Gave us the definition of rhetoric. Outlined rhetorical proofs.

A highly influential book and well worth reading in a good translation.

Hermagoras of Temnos

The Art of Rhetoric

Stasis Theory

Discussion of stasis theory

The 7 W's which is a precursor for our Who, What, When, Why formula

© Bildagentur Zoonar GmbH/Shutterstock.com

Cicero

De Inventione

The **five canons of rhetoric** are discussed:

Inventio (invention)—the discovery and development of your case. The arguments and evidence for your case.
Dispositio (disposition or arrangement)—the arrangement of your speech. This should be done to enhance the persuasive appeal of your speech.
Elocutio (style)—using suitable words to present your case.
Memoria (memory)—memorizing your speech.
Actio (delivery)—graceful regulation of voice and gestures.

© Voronin76/Shutterstock.com

Quintilian claimed that Cicero believed his later works superseded *De Inventione*.

Quintilian

Institutio Oratoria (Institutes of Oratory)

A twelve-volume set that put all of the information on ancient rhetoric in one place.

© Africa Studio/Shutterstock.com

Anonymous

Rhetorica ad Herrenium

Considered the first public speaking textbook.

Also includes the five Canons of Rhetoric. Codified **the Classical Pattern** for organizing a speech:

Exordium—the introduction
Narratio—lay out the case

© Offscreen/Shutterstock.com

Divisio—an outline of the main points to be discussed
Confirmatio—the arguments for the case
Confutatio—attacks arguments against the case
Conclusio—the conclusion

Tells us that there are three reasons why people would speak:

- **Demonstrativum**—praise or condemnation of a person
- **Deliberativum**—a policy speech
- **Ludiciale**—legal controversies spoken to

After looking at this brief summary of six important ancient texts a question comes to mind:

Progymnasmata of Aphthonius of Antioch

4th Century CE

This book contains fourteen exercises for the beginning speaker. The speaker was to master these fourteen exercises and in doing so would be able to deliver effective speeches.

A student should:

- Master the five canons of rhetoric.
- Know the rules of speech so s/he can break them successfully.
- Understand the techniques of public speaking so as to become a knowledgeable consumer of public speaking.
- Effectively use argument.
- Always keep the audience in mind.

In order to be a good public speaker you need something to talk about and you need a way of putting that something together so it makes sense and is persuasive. The ancient teachers of rhetoric devised a series of exercises that would allow students to do just that. These exercises are called the Progymnasmata.

- From the Greek
  - *Pro* means "before"
  - *Gymnasmata* means "exercises"

The Progymnasmata exercises introduced the student of rhetoric to the basic 'stuff' of speeches. The exercises were intended to help the student create and perform complete speeches. We know what they are because four ancient manuscripts devoted to these exercises are available to us to study. The most popular one was written about the fifth century CE and was used during the Renaissance to teach public speaking. We will discuss the Progymnasmata in greater detail later in the text.

CHAPTER 2

Beginning with Aristotle

© Everett Historical/Shutterstock.com

Before we get to the Progymnasmata, we need some background in the practical skills of rhetoric. Sticking with our theme of understanding public speaking the way the ancient rhetoricians did we will now spend some time with Aristotle.

Aristotle has a formula for critiquing or at least understanding public address. It is simple and straightforward. Consequently, knowing it is helpful to you when you go about constructing your speeches. The formula is:

- ❏ Speaker
- ❏ Audience
- ❏ Occasion
- ❏ Speech

Of course things are always more complicated than they look. When constructing or critiquing a speech there are questions that need to be asked. The critic or the speaker asks:

- Why am I giving this speech? What do I hope to accomplish by this speech?
  - What prompted the speech?
  - Was there some outside agency or emergency? (This is sometimes called exigency.)
- To whom am I giving the speech?
  - Why did I choose this audience for this speech?
  - Who is the audience who was chosen for me?
- When and where am I giving this speech?
  - What is the historical/cultural context of the speech?
  - What time of day is the speech given?
  - What is the venue?

The point here is to make sure that you are giving the right speech to the right audience at the right time and place. The critic or speaker wants to make sure of this too. The person critiquing a speech will draw conclusions based on the answers to decide whether the speech has been effective.

For the purposes of constructing an effective speech the speaker needs to look at these four elements and analyze them. Let's break this down so we can figure out what we need to know. After we learn this we can begin putting our own speeches together.

Speaker

That's you and of course *whoever* is giving a speech. So what do you need to know about yourself that will help you create and deliver your speech? Ask yourself these questions to help you along:

- What are my beliefs, attitudes, values, and behaviors?
  - How will these inform my speech?
  - How can I use these to help me be a better speaker?
- What do I already know about the world around me?
- What am I interested in?
- What do I know about my topic before I start doing research?
- Is what I know accurate?
- How am I like or unlike my audience?

© Diego Cervo/Shutterstock.com

As a speaker you have to have good sense, good moral character, and goodwill in order to be successful. Here are some things you need to do as well.

- You need to have a purpose. If you don't know why you are speaking the audience is not going to know either.
- You need ethics. You need to speak on what you believe and construct ethical arguments that allow the audience to want to change.

- ❏ You need ethical source material.
- ❏ You need to tell the audience where you got the material (even if that is in a handout or program and not in the speech proper) and
- ❏ You need to use your proofs ethically.

Audience

Since your job as a speaker is to encourage the audience to move from point A to point B—meaning that you are trying to help the audience think, believe, or do something different than it currently thinks, believes, or does—you have to know who the audience is. Remember that you want to move them to a more truthful, just, and/or ethical position. In order to do so you need to know who they are.

© bikeriderlondon/Shutterstock.com

Since every facet of a speech is informed by the audience to whom it is given you have to ask and answer some questions:

- ❏ What stance should I take on my topic with this audience?
- ❏ How should I compose and practice my speech for this audience?
- ❏ How should I deliver my speech to this audience?

Audiences are not homogeneous. Even in a highly partisan audience division exists. Generally audiences can be divided into three groups:

- ❏ People who agree with you (partisans)
- ❏ People who have no opinion or don't care (neutrals)
- ❏ People who disagree with you (opponents)

The need to know who makes up these divisions, and the extent to which these divisions exist within a given audience, is what drives audience analysis. Knowing who your audience is constitutes the single, most important aspect of good public address.

Audiences also come in different types. It is up to you to know which of these types makes up your complete audience and how you will speak to each in your speech. And yes, you have no control over the first type of audience.

- ❏ The Hit and Run Audience
  - ▪ People who pause to listen and then move on
  - ▪ An example of this is students passing a classroom and stopping to hear a bit of a speech that is being delivered to the class
  - ▪ The speech is not intended for these people
  - ▪ What mischief can result from this type of audience hearing bits of your speech?
- ❏ The Agenda-Oriented Audience
  - ▪ Listens to accomplish its own goals
  - ▪ Not necessarily interested in the persuasive intent of the speaker

- The Voluntary Audience
    - These people come of their own accord
    - But they come for different reasons
    - This audience can be:
        - Homogeneous: alike in thought
        - Heterogeneous: all over the map
        - Hostile: disagree with you
- The Thoughtful Audience
    - These people have come because they want to hear your speech
    - They are not necessarily willing to act on what you say
- The Pro-You Audience
    - They agree with you or they like you
    - They want to engage with you or your topic in some way

So how do you get to know your audience? There are a couple of different ways and a good speaker will use them to get to know the audience as intimately as possible. So let's start with the basics, with a demographic study of audience. **Demography** is the study of populations. For our purposes it is a study of group characteristics.

Looking at any given audience what characteristics do the people in that audience have?

- Ethnicity
- Gender
- Age
- Ability/Disability
- Economic Status
- Education
- Marital Status
- Religion
- Group Affiliation
- Region/Geography
- Culture

© Rawpixel.com/Shutterstock.com

This is not an exhaustive list. There are many other characteristics embodied in specific audiences. Why is this information important?

- Topic choice depends on it
- What you choose from the Progymnasmata depends on it
- Language choices depend on it
- The arguments you make depend on it
- In fact everything depends on it

Each individual audience member has needs and values, attitudes and beliefs that are not captured by a demographic study. A needs analysis of your audience can uncover the beliefs, values, and needs of the audience, thus allowing you to compose an effective speech. Such an analysis looks at internal characteristics of members of the audience.

© Raywoo/Shutterstock.com

A needs analysis would look at the following internal characteristics:

- Spiritual Needs—the need for transcendence
- Social Needs—the need to be with people and be liked and accepted
- Intellectual Needs—the need to appear smart; the need to exercise your brain
- Physical—the need to move; the need to participate in activities; the need for sexual gratification
- Emotional—the need to feel loved and to belong
- Security—the need to feel safe
- Biological—the need to eat, sleep, breathe, etc.

Knowing what your audience needs gives you an idea of what arguments to make or information to give that particular audience.

It is also important to analyze your audience using the following two criteria:

- Time of Day
- Environment

This is called Situational Analysis.

© marekuliasz/Shutterstock.com

A person's reaction to information may be influenced by the time of day at which it is encountered. You will notice, if you read the papers, that many crimes take place between midnight and 6:00 a.m. There is a reason for that. People react differently to stimuli at different times of the day. The prank of toilet-papering your professor's house sounds hilarious at 3:00 a.m., but not so hilarious at 7:00 p.m. We hang out at 9:00 p.m., but not necessarily at 9:00 a.m.

- Can your audience feel comfortable with a speech about serial killers during your 8:00 a.m. speech class?
- Can your audience listen to your speech on yummy food at 2:00 p.m. when no one has had lunch?

Biological clocks play a role here as well. Some people are more alert at 8:00 a.m., some at 10:00 p.m.

- Where does your audience fall in this regard?
- Are they morning or evening people?
- Is the time at which your speech is given an "up" or "down" time for your audience?

The environment in which the speech is given will also affect your audience. Students frequently wish to give speeches outside. But that is always problematic. The open air, the noise, the monumental distraction of people walking by have a negative effect on the audience. You should consider all of these things before you decide on an outside venue. Of course indoors has its disadvantages as well.

Here are some things to consider when speaking indoors:
- How big is the room?
- Do I have adequate technology?
- Where will people be sitting?
- Is the lighting adequate?
- Is a podium available?
- What are the sightlines like? Can I be seen?
- How close am I to the audience?
- What are the acoustics like in the room?
    - Will people have trouble hearing me?
    - Are there hearing devices for those who want them?

© improvize/Shutterstock.com

How do you do audience analysis in everyday situations? After all most of us don't have armies of pollsters to do this analysis for us. So what is helpful for us? Well we can ask and answer the following questions:

- What is the organization/group/business I am speaking to?
- Who is likely to join such an organization/group or be employed by the business?
- Who from the organization/group/business is likely to be at my speech?
    - What does this audience look like (demographics)?
    - Are they there because they want to be or they have to be?
    - What does this audience already know about the topic?
    - Why is the audience at my speech?
- What time of day is the speech to be given?
- Where will I be giving my speech?

© Rawpixel/Shutterstock.com

That is just a starter list. There are many more questions you can ask that will help you do audience analysis in the real world.

To be successful as a speechmaker you need to help the audience be part of what's happening. You have to persuade the audience to identify with each other and with you and come to a common understanding of the message.

- Remember that each person in the audience has his/her own beliefs, attitudes, values, and behaviors.
- People will listen to the speech through these filters.

- ❏ Knowing what your audience members already think is important.
- ❏ Your speech has to appeal to a diverse audience.
    - ▪ You do this by choosing a good topic and
    - ▪ By using arguments that reinforce partisans, lure neutrals, and make opponents stop and think about the topic.

Occasion

The occasion for your speech is the where and why of speaking. It contains the following elements:

- ❏ The reason why you are speaking
- ❏ The place in which you will speak
- ❏ The time of day at which you will speak
- ❏ The history of this occasion

© jokerpro/Shutterstock.com

Why is it important to take these elements into account? Let's see:

The reason why you are speaking affects your audience analysis, your topic choice, and various other elements of the speechmaking process.

- ❏ Is this an informative, persuasive, or ceremonial speech?
    - ▪ Is this a fact, policy, or values speech?
    - ▪ How long should the speech be?
    - ▪ Is this a formal or informal occasion?
    - ▪ Are there rules for speaking at this event?

The place in which you speak. The venue for the speech affects tone, word choice, example choice, and visual aid choice among other considerations.

The time of day in which you speak. The time of day affects topic choice, audience analysis, example choice, and other aspects of speechmaking.

The history of this occasion.

- ❏ What happens before you speak?
- ❏ Is there a dinner or other speeches or videos or just chatting before or after your speech?
- ❏ If this is an ongoing event, what speeches have been given in prior years?
- ❏ How long should the speech be? What are the expectations of speech length in this venue?
- ❏ Who spoke last year and what did that person say?
- ❏ Who is speaking just prior to your speech and what did that person say?
- ❏ How long have the speeches been prior to your address?

Answering all of the questions posed above will allow you to craft a speech that meets the needs of the audience and the occasion for which that audience has come together.

Speech

The speech itself is made up of the exercises you will be practicing in class. The Progymnasmata was designed to "fill-in-the-blanks" of the basic speech outline.

© R. Gino Santa Maria/Shutterstock.com

Remember from Chapter 1 that Corax was the first rhetorician to outline a speech. His outline looks like this:

- Introduction
    - Tell the audience what you will be arguing
    - Begin outlining your credibility
    - Give the audience a reason to listen
- Narration
    - Discuss your argument
    - Give the audience an understanding of the topic
- Confirmation
    - Why you take the position you take
    - Arguments for the proposition
- Confutation
    - Explain the counter-arguments
    - Explain why these arguments are weak
- Peroration
    - Leave the audience with a reason to side with you
    - Strong closing statements increase your credibility

This outline can also be seen in the *Rhetorica ad Herrenium* as:

- Exordium—the introduction
- Narratio—lay out the case
- Divisio—explaining the main points
- Confirmatio—the arguments for the case
- Refutatio—attacks arguments against the case
- Conclusio—the conclusion

This outline is the one (with a few additions or deletions) that is still used by most speakers in twenty-first century America. Note that this outline is concerned with persuasion no matter what the general purpose of the speech is. There is a good deal of leeway in this outline which allows for the speaker to craft a speech that is unique to him/her so don't feel trapped by this organization. It is more flexible than it looks.

The important point regarding these outlines is that the speech needs to be organized or you will not achieve your persuasive goal.

If you were going to critique a speech using Aristotle's four-part division, you would answer the following questions in regard to the speech itself:

- How does the speech meet the demands of the occasion?
- How does the speech take the audience into account?
- What language does the speaker use to make his/her points?
- If the speaker is using visual aids, do those visual aids enhance or detract from the speech?
- What arguments does the speaker make?
    - Are those arguments effective?
    - Do the arguments actually make the case?
- What supporting materials does the speaker use?
    - Are they effective?
    - Do they support the argument?
- Is the speaker ethical in her/his use of evidence?

Actually these questions are profitable to ask when composing a speech. If you keep these questions in mind you are more likely to compose an effective speech.

CHAPTER 3

Roll Out the Canons

© Ilya Zonov/Shutterstock.com

You will recall from earlier in the text that **The Rhetorica ad Herrenium** was one of the first public speaking textbook. It, along with Cicero's *De Inventione,* contains the five canons of rhetoric that are still used today. These canons were developed to help citizen-speakers learn the craft of rhetorical discourse. They represent a system or a "how to" guide that helps the citizen speaker in two ways:

- ❏ The citizen-speaker can use them to develop an effective speech
- ❏ The citizen-speaker can use them to critique a speech

Here are the canons.

Inventio (Invention)

The first canon is called invention because this is the stage at which you "discover" your case and develop the arguments and evidence for it. In other words you figure out what you are going to say and then look for arguments to support your specific purpose. The ancient rhetoricians favored asking a question and then answering it as a means to develop the case and then argue for it. By asking the question you can then search for the arguments that will most effectively move the audience to think, believe, or do what you wish them to think, believe, or do.

© Martina Osmy/Shutterstock.com

Aristotle gave the first list of questions, which he called *topoi,* or topics of invention, but feel free to ask yourself other types of questions.

- ❏ Definition. What is it?
- ❏ Comparison. How are these things the same?
- ❏ Contrast. How are things different?
- ❏ Cause and effect. Does one thing cause another?
- ❏ Conjecture. This is what you think has happened or will happen. Conspiracy theories are conjecture.

Answer these questions for yourself as you work through invention:
- ❏ What broad category of question am I asking?
- ❏ What do I want the audience to think, believe, or do by the time my speech is over?
- ❏ Who is my audience?
- ❏ Depending on the time of day and the history of the audience what are my best choices for arguments?
- ❏ How do I include a good mix of ethos, pathos, and logos arguments?
- ❏ What is the occasion and how does it affect what arguments I choose?
- ❏ Which of the stasis questions should I be using for this speech?
    - ▪ Policy
    - ▪ Fact
    - ▪ Value

Dispositio (Disposition or Arrangement)

In modern parlance this is called organization. All speeches need an organizational structure. If your speech is not organized, your audience will not be able to follow your argument. A disorganized speech hurts your credibility. Remember, part of your ethos (character) is derived from what the audience learns about you during the speech. If you are disorganized, one of the things they learn about you is uncomplimentary—the audience will believe you are not competent.

© bikeriderlondon/Shutterstock.com

Here are two ways one might organize a speech.

Modern Organizational Pattern

Introduction:
    Attention-getter: engage the audience
    Credibility: why you are qualified to speak on this subject
    Why Should I Listen?: tell the audience how it can benefit from listening to the speech.
    Thesis: what you will speak about
    Preview: tell the audience what your main points are
    Transition: seamlessly move to your first main point

Main Point number 1: Support the central idea/thesis
    Sub-points
    Make your arguments
    Summarize the argument
    Transition: seamlessly move to your next main point

© Valerie Potapova/Shutterstock.com

Main Point number 2: Support the central idea/thesis
    Sub-points
    Make your arguments
    Summarize the argument
    Transition: seamlessly move to your next main point

Main Point number 3: Support the central idea/thesis
    Sub-points
    Make your arguments
    Summarize the argument
    Transition: seamlessly move to your conclusion

Conclusion
    Summary: Remind your audience what your speech was about
    Call to action: encourage the audience to do something about what you said
    Clincher: strong closing statement that lets the audience know you are finished

Classical Pattern

Introduction
    Credibility
    Topic

Narration
    Stasis: what is the ground from which you are arguing?
    Support the thesis
    Transition

© ArchMan/Shutterstock.com

Confirmation
Arguments for your case
Support for your arguments
This is where all your supporting material comes in

Refutation
Addresses arguments against your case
This is where you acknowledge these and defend against them

Conclusion
Make sure you have a strong closing

Within these arrangements a speaker needs to organize his/her main points.

Such organization includes:

- Chronological: organized sequentially. Time, process
- Spatially: organized directionally. Top to bottom, left to right
- Causal: organized to show cause and effect
- Problem-Solution: organized by parts. Outline the problem. Offer a solution
- Topical: all purpose organization. Use subtopics for main points

© Alis Leonte/Shutterstock.com

Elocutio (Style)

The ancients understood elocutio to be "using suitable words to present your case." What words you choose and how you craft sentences using those words is important to good speech-making. That importance stems from three things:

- the difference between writing for reading purposes and writing for speaking purposes,
- the need to be understood, and
- the need to say exactly what you want to say to a particular audience.

Public speaking is not the same as writing, so speakers should use a heightened form of their everyday word choice not the more formal language used in, say, an essay for an English composition class. We write our speeches out if we are crafting them the old-fashioned way. But if we write them to be read rather than spoken aloud, we run into trouble. The trouble is that the audience will get lost in big words and phrases. The speech will sound like an essay and not like a talk that personally addresses individual members of the audience. Your speeches should be written and delivered in what is called oral style.

Oral style is direct, personal, and more informal than formal. It is not however, so informal that you can speak using the same language you do when speaking to your friends.

Some things to think about concerning oral style:

- Use personal pronouns.
- Use active verbs.
- Formal construction like "It is to be hoped" can be used in writing, but sound stilted and uninteresting in speaking.
- Use vocal phrasing to indicate thought units.
- Use short thought units. Long sentences are difficult to follow and the audience may give up.
- AVOID:
  - Jargon
  - Colorful metaphors. In other words, swearing.
  - Undefined technical terms.
  - Slang

Memoria (Memory)

The ancients encouraged their students to memorize their speeches. We no longer do this, but there is nothing stopping you from trying this if you think it will add to the persuasive impact of your message.

© Kjpargeter/Shutterstock.com

Other methods of delivery include:

- ❏ Manuscript
    - a speech written in its entirety and delivered word-for-word from this written page
- ❏ Extemporaneous
    - speaking from notes, outline, or bullet points

For formal occasions many modern speakers use a manuscript. You would think that is easy as you have the words right in front of you, but it isn't.

- ❏ Upside of using a manuscript
    - Allows crafting of the speech
    - Helps prevent the speaker from saying something s/he doesn't mean to say
    - Keeps the speaker on track with arguments. No tangents
    - Makes it easier to adhere to time limits
- ❏ Downside of using a manuscript
    - Dependence on manuscript can negatively affect delivery
    - Speech may sound canned
    - Unless the speaker has practiced extensively with the manuscript s/he will not be able to respond to audience

Many speakers today use teleprompters. These devices allow a speaker to make maximum eye contact with the audience and still use a manuscript. In some ways this is the best of both worlds as the speaker can craft an artful speech and look as if s/he is speaking either from memory or extemporaneously.

Extemporaneous speaking is the use of notes or an outline rather than a manuscript.

- ❏ Upside of doing extemporaneous speaking
    - Allows for maximum interaction with the audience
    - Allows for quick response to the audience
    - Shows confidence
- ❏ Downside of doing extemporaneous speaking
    - Difficult to carry off effectively for beginning speakers
    - Difficult to craft a speech unless one knows a good deal about the topic
    - Difficult to adhere to time limits

You, as a speaker, must decide for yourself what method you will use: memory, manuscript, or extemporaneous for your speech.

Actio (Delivery)

This canon deals with the graceful regulation of voice and gestures. For modern speakers we can add the manipulation of visual aids to this list.

© Khakimullin Aleksandr/Shutterstock.com

Let's tackle voice first. You do not have to be like Demosthenes who filled his mouth with pebbles and shouted at the sea to train his voice. But you do have to know how the voice works so that you can use it like the instrument it is, to its best effect.

Voice

Your voice is the instrument you use to "play your speech." Think of using your voice for speech-making as you use a guitar, a piano, or a bass to make music.

© ollyy/Shutterstock.com

Part of your credibility derives from how your audience reacts to your voice. A pleasing voice encourages the audience to listen to you. By pleasing I mean a voice the audience likes—deep or high, strong or sweet—it doesn't matter as long as it is attractive to the audience. Think Morgan Freeman, James Earl Jones.

Here is what you have to know about your voice in order to be able to use it to your best ability:

- **Volume:** loudness/softness of the voice
    - Volume conveys emotion
    - Volume is regulated by the size of the room
    - Volume is affected by the technology you use

- **Rate:** the speed at which you speak
    - Generally between 100–150 words per minute
    - Rate conveys emotion
    - Rate can be used to emphasize a point
    - Rate should change during the speech in reaction to the audience and the content of the speech

- **Pausing:** this is the punctuation of speech
    - Pausing gives the audience time to mentally relax
    - It separates thought units
    - Incorrect pausing can change the meaning of a sentence or thought unit

- **Pitch:** the range of the voice
    - Most people have a two-octave pitch range for their speaking voices
    - Your voice runs from low (James Earl Jones) to high (Minnie Mouse)
    - Conveys emotion
    - Helps with characterization when telling stories, quoting others
    - Using pitch keeps you from being monotone

❏ **Vocal Variety**: sometimes called intonation, inflection, or melody. This is a combination of all of the above aspects and also includes cadence—the rise and fall of the voice when speaking.

And then there is:

❏ **Articulation:** the correct formations of sounds. Articulation is what produces our accents. Every language has established and correct ways of articulating the sounds that make up the words of that language. Poor articulation leads to a loss of credibility. Over-articulating can do the same thing.
- Your accent can work for you if you want to use it.
- If your accent has articulation that is difficult for others to understand think about altering your word choice to be more readily understood.
- Audiences can stereotype you based on your accent. Be aware of that.

❏ **Pronunciation:** the correct formation of words. Mispronouncing words is the fastest way to lose credibility there is. Mispronunciation indicates to the audience that you have not bothered to look up words you don't know and have not bothered to practice your speech.

Gestures

There is no one "right way" to deliver a speech non-verbally. You are an individual and you must find the right way for you. Some people are comfortable gesturing, some people not. Some people are comfortable behind a podium, some people not. Some people feel comfortable using movement, some people not. Additionally, the topic you choose and the way you approach that topic will influence how you use your body to convey meaning.

© ostill/Shutterstock.com

There are some things to avoid however:

- ❏ Tapping the podium
- ❏ Leaning on the podium
- ❏ Pacing aimlessly
- ❏ Avoiding eye contact
- ❏ Putting your hands in your pockets
- ❏ Touching your face
- ❏ Putting your hands behind your back
- ❏ Playing with your hair
- ❏ Staring at your PowerPoint
- ❏ Chewing gum
- ❏ Bringing a pencil up with you and playing with it

You get the picture. All these things are distracting. They hurt your credibility and therefore your success as a speaker.

Appearance

Looking prepared, polished, and confident is important. Dressing appropriately for the occasion and the topic of your speech is a must. From the time you enter the room to the time you leave the audience will be watching you. Part of your credibility comes from how they judge your appearance and demeanor. Some things to think about:

- Look attentive and be engaged in the occasion before your speech
- Approach the podium with confidence
- Make sure your speech is in order
- Don't fumble with notes or manuscript
- Depart from the podium with confidence
- Ask about the dress code and stick to it unless it will interfere with your speech
- Make sure your clothes fit
    - Clothes that are too tight make you look and the audience feel uncomfortable
    - Clothes that are too loose make you look too small
    - Make sure your underclothes are not visible
    - Make sure your clothes are clean and pressed
    - Choose colors carefully as they have an effect on the audience
    - Make sure your shoes are comfortable and safe
    - Do not wear distracting jewelry and other artifacts

Visual Aids

So, the ancient Greeks didn't have access to the kinds of visual aids we have today, but they did understand that sometimes showing people a thing is more persuasive than simply talking about it. In fact some speeches lose all possibility of being persuasive, not to say meaningful, if visual aids are not used.

Visual aids are needed when:

- Definitions are important
- Numbers play a role in your argument
- Demonstrating a thing makes a stronger point than talking about it
- You want audience participation beyond listening
- Descriptions need a boost

Here is a list of typical visual aids
- PowerPoint
- Prezi
- Videos
- Photographs
- Lists
- Graphs

- Charts
- Objects
- People
- Animals

This is not an exhaustive list, but it does indicate a couple of things. You should

- Prepare the visual aids before you deliver your speech
- Practice with them before you deliver your speech
- Be sure the objects you are using are easy to handle
- Make sure beforehand, that if you need audience participation, there are people in the audience willing to help
- Know how to use the technology available to you at the speech venue
- Have a back-up if the technology fails you before or during your speech
- Remember that animals are unpredictable. Your parrot may not talk or your dog may not do its tricks at the appropriate time in your speech.

Visual aids must be clean, polished, and professional-looking. For example, using a chalk or white board may indicate to the audience that you are not prepared. If your handwriting is poor your credibility is in danger. The expectation that visual aids will be professional-looking is high today because of the belief that everyone has access to the Internet and knows how to use it. Part of your credibility rests on this expectation. Be aware. Be very aware.

CHAPTER 4

Let's Argue

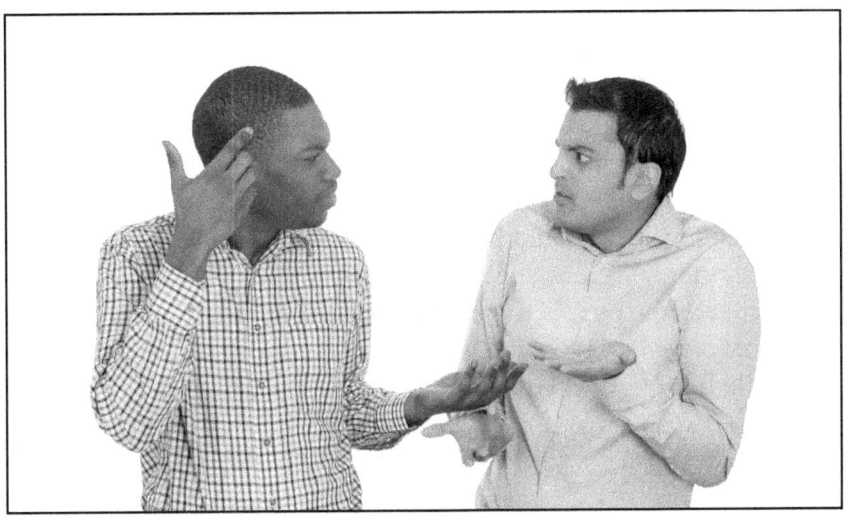

Introduction

If we agree that all rhetoric is persuasive then we need to know about argumentation. Arguments come in two flavors—**Artistic** and **Inartistic** or if you prefer **Intrinsic** and **Extrinsic**. You will need both types in most of the speaking that you do. Beyond this division you have to decide whether you are arguing **fact, policy, or value** and how you are going to fit this two-part division into that. So let's look at argumentation and see what we find.

This chapter will help you learn how to make arguments that will encourage the audience to think, believe, or do what you are hoping they will by the end of your speech. We will start by looking at how to develop the premise or purpose for your speeches.

- ❏ In classical rhetoric speeches were categorized in the following ways:
    - Forensic or legal
    - Deliberative or policy/legislative
    - Epideictic or ceremonial

❏ In modern times we divide speaking into:
- Informative
- Persuasive
- Ceremonial

❏ These three types of speeches will tell you what the general purpose of your speech is:
- Informative speeches inform on a topic
- Persuasive speeches argue for a position on an issue
- Ceremonial speeches fulfill a role in the rituals of our time

Now, you are probably asking, "if the ancient rhetoricians believed that all rhetoric was persuasive, then isn't the general purpose of any speech persuasive?"

The answer to that last question is in a general sense 'yes.' But remember that your general speech purpose is not the only purpose of your speech. Once you settle on your general purpose your next task is to choose a specific speech purpose. It is at this point that the speech becomes not only persuasive but also informative or ceremonial.

❏ The specific purpose should let you, and the audience, know what particular aspect of a topic you will cover in your speech.
❏ The specific speech purpose should indicate which of the three categories—informative, persuasive, or ceremonial—your speech falls into.
❏ If your general speech purpose is to persuade then the specific speech purpose should tell the audience what type of speech you will give: fact, value, or policy and what you want the audience to think, believe, or do by the time the speech is over.

Once you get that purpose down you need to figure out how to argue your point. Ancient rhetoricians suggest that there are two general types of arguments:

❏ Artistic or Intrinsic Proofs—these are arguments that the speaker invents
❏ Inartistic or Extrinsic Proofs—these are arguments that the speakers finds

So what does that all mean? Let's find out.

Artistic Arguments

Artistic arguments are arguments that the speaker **invents** and their source is the speaker. Aristotle divided these arguments into three categories.

ETHOS—These are credibility arguments. Ideas, arguments, and information are connected to the people or entities that represent them. If the person carrying the idea is considered untrustworthy, then the speech has a long way to go to get the audience to move closer to the speaker's position. The character of the person may encourage

© wacpan/Shutterstock.com

the audience to be skeptical or even hostile to the ideas presented. On the other hand, if the person is trustworthy then the audience will be more likely to approve the argument.

- ❏ Aristotle believed that ethos is the strongest argument. If you trust a person you are likely to do what s/he asks without thinking through the logic of the request.
- ❏ Aristotle suggested that the speaker brings this to the audience:
  - Demonstrated wisdom about social truths
  - Excellence or competence
  - Evidence of good intent
- ❏ Ethos is a continuum. Ethos either builds or deteriorates during the speech. The speaker hopes to finish the speech with a higher degree of credibility (ethos) than when the speech began.
  - **Prior Ethos**—what you bring to the situation and what the audience already knows about you.
    - Reputation. What is the speaker's reputation in the world outside of this particular speaking event?
    - Appearance. Does the speaker look like s/he knows what s/he is talking about? Dressed appropriately? Confident approach/departure from the podium?
    - Introduction. What was said about the speaker before the speech began? Does the introduction enhance the speaker's reputation?
    - Occasion. Why is the speaker speaking at this occasion?
    - Context. Where and when is the speech given?
  - **Continuing Ethos**—what happens during the speech
    - Expertise. Does the speaker know the subject matter of the speech?
    - Trustworthiness. Is the speaker telling the truth?
    - Dynamism. Is the speaker interested in the speech? The audience? The occasion?
    - Identification. Can I, as an audience member, identify with the speaker? Is the speaker talking at me or to me?
    - Derived ethos from good use of sources. Is the speaker using credible sources and using them honestly?
  - **Terminal Ethos**—what you end up with
    - Ask, was the speech successful?
    - Did the speaker have a strong conclusion?
    - Did the speaker depart the podium well? Does the speaker still look interested in the occasion? Is the speaker still engaged?

The ancient understanding of ethos was that an individual's ethos resided in the community not in the individual. You get your reputation from the people around you. Even if you are a great person if the community does not agree, you have negative credibility. We are not as likely to believe that these days. We think ethos resides in the person. But in fact, since what we know of people is what others say about that person (unless the person is personally known to us) then we are not so very different from the ancient Greeks. Think about any celebrity: that celebrity's ethos is derived not from our personal knowledge but from what the culture at large says about him/her.

PATHOS—These are arguments that appeal to the audience's beliefs, attitudes, values, and needs. Audience analysis is essential if you are to use these arguments effectively. Pathos arguments appeal to an audience's beliefs, attitudes, values, and needs. At their core, they are arguments that tap emotion rather than reason. Therefore, pathos arguments should not be a speaker's sole line of argument. Below are the three categories of Pathos Appeals.

- Appeals to emotion
  - Persuasive impact to well-reasoned arguments
  - Can be to positive or negative emotions
  - Examples of appeals to emotion:
    - Humane Society TV advertisements featuring abused and neglected animals
    - Feed the hungry TV advertisements featuring hungry children
  - Good pathos appeals
    - Carefully choose language
    - Avoid inflammatory examples
    - Use good supporting materials

- Appeals to need
  - Runs the gamut. Safety, security, physical, spiritual, emotional, social, love, worthiness, et al.
  - Again, watch the ethics. Don't try to manufacture a need when one is clearly not there.
  - Examples of appeal to needs:
    - Home security advertisements
    - Almost any advertisement for exercise equipment or dieting. These appeal to love and belongingness needs as well as self-esteem needs.

- Appeals to values are defined as "enduring beliefs"
  - Tell us how to behave, who we are, what we believe, etc.
  - Values grow out of needs and are influenced by culture.
  - Values help us decide what is worthy of persuasion.
  - They help us decide what needs to be changed and what needs to stay the same.
  - Examples of value needs:
    - Patriotic appeals
    - Advertisements to help the less fortunate are not only appeals to emotion they can also be appeals to the values of compassion and responsibility for others.

LOGOS— Logic appeals that use reasoning to mediate change. This is done in a number of different ways. Examples are:

- Inductive Reasoning: reason from specific to general.
  - Because one teenager crashes his/her car you make the argument that most or all teenagers are unsafe drivers.

- Deductive Reasoning (The Sherlock Holmes Method): reason from general to specific.
  - Because most teenagers are unsafe drivers 17-year-old Taylor will be an unsafe driver.

- Causation: two events are shown to be in relation to one another—one causing the other.
  - Drinking too much alcohol causes impaired driving

- ❏ Parallel Case: what happens in one case will happen in a similar situation.
  - ◁ Alcohol was consumed at the Middle Valley High School prom after-party so alcohol will be consumed at the Wendell Wilkie High School after-party.

- ❏ Analogy: If two things are alike in certain ways that can be seen, they will be alike in certain ways that cannot be seen.
  - ◁ Alcohol and marijuana are alike in their mind-altering properties so they are alike in their effects on people's lives.

Inartistic Arguments

These are the arguments that you **find** to support the point you wish to make. For people like Aristotle inartistic proofs were things like contracts, testimony, and other sources that exist outside the speaker. In today's language we call these proofs supporting materials. The ethical speaker chooses appropriate source materials that supports the argument the speaker makes.

Appropriate source materials include but are not limited to:

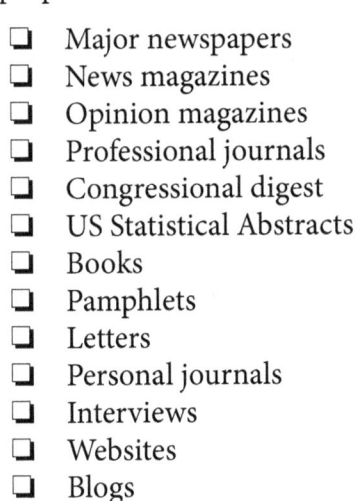

- ❏ Major newspapers
- ❏ News magazines
- ❏ Opinion magazines
- ❏ Professional journals
- ❏ Congressional digest
- ❏ US Statistical Abstracts
- ❏ Books
- ❏ Pamphlets
- ❏ Letters
- ❏ Personal journals
- ❏ Interviews
- ❏ Websites
- ❏ Blogs

© Stuart Miles/Shutterstock.com

Detecting Bias

All source material has a bias. Sometimes the bias is explicit—people come right out and tell you where they stand—and sometimes you have to hunt for it. Regardless of which it is bias is always present. We have a tendency not to see bias when the bias affirms what we believe. That is when we need to be careful.

How do we detect bias? By asking the following questions:

Statistics

- ❏ **What do the statistics tell us?**
  - ◁ Does the statistic actually prove the point the source is trying to make?
- ❏ **How does the source use statistics?**
  - ◁ Does the source show all the numbers of a given poll or study or just the ones that make the source's case?

Photography

- **How does the source use photographs?**
  - Photograph placement. Where a photograph appears in a source will influence how you understand the subject of the photograph.
  - Photograph choice. Look at these two photographs of Detroit, MI. They tell completely different stories.

© Atomazul/Shutterstock.com   © Marina Mikhaylova/Shutterstock.com

- **Have you heard of the term "fauxtography?"** This term means "fake photography." Call it photoshopping if you like. It is done to make a point and influence audience.
  - It's done by cropping photographs to leave out important images
  - It's done by adding new elements to the image
  - Look at this example: This is Charles Dickens. He looks great on the left, yes? That was the work of Matthew Brady. He touched up the photo to make Dickens look better. And this was done in 1867! Search "faked photos" online and see what is happening today.

Source: Public Domain

Story Placement

- **Where are stories placed?** Where stories are placed in a newspaper or magazine has an impact on which people think about them.
    - Headline stories are considered more important
    - Stories that lead news shows are considered most important
    - Stories can be "buried" by keeping them off the front page

- **Which stories are run?** By choosing some stories over others people in the media choose for the public which stories will be considered noteworthy and which will not.
    - During John Kennedy's presidency there was a "gentlemen's agreement" among reporters not to publish anything about the president's extra-marital affairs. President Bill Clinton had no such agreement.

Headlines

- **What does the headline say?** "Headless body in Topless Bar" is considered one of the all-time best headlines. But what does it tell you about the actual facts of the story? For example, there is still a bit of controversy surrounding the nature of the bar. Was it really a topless bar? Is the headline too good to check on the nature of the bar and find out the truth?
    - Sometimes the headline doesn't have much to do with the actual story. Sometimes it pulls out the sensational at the expense of real understanding.

In 2014, Governor Jan Brewer of Arizona, vetoed state Senate Bill 1062 these headlines appeared in various news organs:

- The *Washington Post*: "Brewer Kills Bill Allowing Refusal to Serve Gays"
- *USA Today*: "Arizona Governor Vetoes Anti-Gay Bill"
- *Yahoo News*: "Arizona Governor Vetoes Controversial Anti-Gay, 'Religious Freedom' Bill"
- The *Week*: "Jan Brewer Vetoes Arizona 'Religious Freedom' Bill"
- The *Wall Street Journal* "Veto Kills Arizona Religious Measure"
- *Politico* "Jan Brewer Vetoes SB 1062"

Each headline promotes a different perception of this issue. Only one of them achieves neutrality.

- The *Washington Post* considers SB 1062 to be a bill that is about discrimination.
- Notice the quotation marks around "Religious Freedom" in the headline in *The Week*. They are scare quotes and are there to indicate that the editors of this news outlet reject the idea that SB 1062 is a bill about religious freedom.
- The *Wall Street Journal* accepts the idea that SB 1062 is essentially a bill to protect the free exercise of religion by business owners.
- The *Politico* is attempting to be as neutral as possible.

So after reading these headlines what would you expect SB 1062 to have said? You can read the bill for yourself by looking it up. If you want to skip that here is a snippet from an article in *Politico*:

Arizona Gov. Jan Brewer on Wednesday vetoed a controversial bill—called by some a religious-freedom bill and others an anti-gay bill...

1. First introduced Jan. 14, and passed by the state Senate 17–13 on Feb. 19, it passed the state House 33–27 on Feb. 20.
2. It would have changed part of an existing Arizona state law regarding free exercise of religion to broaden protections to nongovernmental entities. The bill would have changed the definition of "person" from referring just to a religious institution to include "any individual, association, partnership, corporation, church, religious assembly or institution or other business organization." It also would have added language that says individuals may use burdens on their religious exercise as a defense in judicial actions even if the government is not a part of the case. This essentially means businesses have a right to claim a religious objection to providing services to customers.
3. It set out requirements for what people claiming their religious beliefs are burdened must prove. "1. That the person's action or refusal to act is motivated by a religious belief. 2. That the person's religious belief is sincerely held. 3. That the state action substantially burdens the exercise of the person's religious beliefs." (Kopan)

What this exercise tells us is that you have to read carefully in order to understand headline bias.

Types of Supporting Materials

A lot of this source material is also on the web. Since you are more likely to go to websites for your information than you are hard copy publications we will need to look at how to judge the appropriateness and accuracy of Internet sources. Not everything you find on the Internet is accurate and/or helpful. When researching online think about the following:

- Some search engines are better than others.
- There are many different kinds of websites:
  - Advocacy websites
  - Information websites
  - Personal websites
  - Commercial websites

© Sergey Novikov/Shutterstock.com

Not all of them are equal in the quality of their postings. Just like you have to check for the biases of print media, you have to check for the biases of web-based sources.

- Criteria for evaluating Internet sources:
  - **Authority:** evaluate the credentials of the source and the sponsor of the website.
  - **Accuracy:** look for additional links that also talk about the topic. What do they say?
  - **Objectivity:** Know the bias. Look for mission statements and "About Us" links so you can learn about them. Some websites look harmless but aren't.
  - **Currency:** Date of posting. Must be as up-to-date as possible. This is very important when your topic is time sensitive.
  - **Coverage:** One article cannot give you all the information you need. Good websites will give you places to go to get more information.

When doing research what should you be looking for? Well, it depends on the argument you wish to make. How do you wish to persuade the audience to change? Ideally you will support your artistic arguments with inartistic arguments/evidence. This evidence comes in four types.

Facts
- Data that have been verified by observation
- Facts contain information that can be judged true or false, correct/incorrect
- Types of facts
  - Established facts: data verified consistently by many observations
  - Definitions: these are straightforward and neutral. Do not add opinion to them
  - Descriptions: how something looks, tastes, smells, etc.

Statistics
- Statistics are numerical facts
- Includes: average, mean, percentage, and ratio
- It is your choice in how you present these. But remember that you can change how people view numbers by how you talk about them.
  - Percentages hide real numbers
  - Extremes on either end of the curve can distort averages
  - Polls need to be analyzed to make sure the numbers mean something

Example
- Adds personal touch to the speech
- Types of examples:
  - **Real**: they actually happened. Make sure they are real. Sometimes people make up stories. Check several places to make sure the story is true.
  - **Hypothetical**: didn't really happen but might or could occur. You might combine elements of current airline travel to illustrate the point of how uncomfortable it has become, rather than give a personal example. If your example is hypothetical you must alert the audience to the fact.
  - **Brief**: quick to the point. Such an example could be only one sentence long.
  - **Extended**: also called a narrative. Your entire speech could be one long example/narrative.

Testimony and Quotes
- Citing a qualified source to support your point
- Can do this through direct quote or by paraphrase
- Types of testimony
  - Expert: an expert in the field supports your point
    - Your speech is about *Buffy the Vampire Slayer*. You quote Joss Whedon who is the creator of this TV show.
  - Peer or Lay—has first-hand experience, but not an expert
    - Your speech is about New York Yankees baseball. You quote your friend who is a fan.
  - Prestige: high ethos person supports your point
    - Your speech is about farming. You quote highly respected actress Meryl Streep because she starred in a movie about farming.

You will note, when we get there, that some types of supporting material are the modern equivalent of the Progymnasmata exercises.

CHAPTER 5

Let's Argue Some More

Artistic and inartistic arguments are not the only game in town when it comes to constructing arguments that are truly persuasive. Other aspects of argumentation need to be considered. Here they are.

Stasis

Stasis Theory was first brought to Rome by a rhetoric teacher named Hermagoras. Both Cicero and Quintilian found the concept useful and expanded on it. In Greek *stasis* means literally "strife" and "immobility." In rhetoric it means: **the place or ground of the dispute.** From an argument standpoint, stasis is the place where opposing forces come together.

- All arguments or controversies are based on the grounds of the dispute. Meaning that everyone has to be on the same page or you can't have a decent argument. Before you can begin to argue you have to agree on what you are arguing about.

- ❏ Knowing what the points of disagreement are makes it easier for the speaker to:
  - ▪ formulate arguments for his/her position,
  - ▪ understand the arguments against his/her position,
  - ▪ make a good guess about how the audience can be persuaded.
- ❏ Stasis helps you find which arguments are available to you and which are not.

Stasis also helps you:

- ❏ Clarify your thinking about the dispute
- ❏ Outline what the arguments on both sides of the issue
- ❏ Think about the assumptions and values shared by the audience
- ❏ Realize you need to do more research
- ❏ Understand which proofs or arguments are crucial to your case
- ❏ Arrange your argument

The following questions will help you establish stasis:

- ❏ Conjecture—Does a thing exist? Did it happen?
- ❏ Definition—What kind of thing or event is it?
- ❏ Quality—Is it right or wrong?
- ❏ Policy—What should we do?

These four stasis questions can be further refined by asking general, specific, very specific, theoretical, or practical questions. Below are examples.

- ❏ General: Should people have children?
- ❏ Specific: Should people over fifty-five have children?
- ❏ Very specific: Should Jay and Kateri Schwandt who have more than a dozen children have any more?
- ❏ Theoretical: Will having children cease to be a biological imperative?
- ❏ Practical: Is having children a financial burden?

Knowing how people frame their questions tells you how to respond. It also puts the issue in stasis—the point where you can agree to disagree. So further down the line when you are working on your persuasive speeches you might begin by asking a question that your speech will answer. Perhaps it will be one of these types of stasis questions.

Other Considerations

Status Quo

Status quo is a Latin term that literally translated means "the state in which." In argument it means the current state of the world or the way things are. A speaker may argue for the status quo or against it. Regardless of which argument the speaker makes the speaker must have, with the audience, a shared understanding of the status quo. The status quo is considered to stand unless good arguments can be made for changing it. Which brings us to . . .

© JeremyWhat/Shutterstock.com

Presumption

- A proposition stands good until some sufficient reason is presented that refutes it.
- The status quo is fine until proven otherwise.

Burden of Proof

This term refers to the requirement that those wishing to change the status quo offer reasons why it should be changed.

The burden of proving that what is being suggested is better than what exists rests with the person asking for the change. When arguing for change the speaker has to overcome the natural desire of people to keep things as they are.

Arguing Facts

As mentioned previously, a fact is an observable truth. You argue for a fact by showing, through evidence, that something is either true or false.

An argument of fact might establish:

- Something as factual or
- That given the evidence something could be true.

We do not argue over obvious established facts. The fact that water is wet and the sun rises in the east does not need to be argued. But there are facts that need to be established and are not obvious. The facts surrounding some of the most contentious issues of the day are precisely the kinds of facts that need thorough analysis and debate.

- Hydraulic fracturing
  - What is it?
  - Does it do harm to the environment?
  - Does it create jobs?

- Death Penalty
  - What is it?
  - Does it deter crime?
  - Is it constitutional?

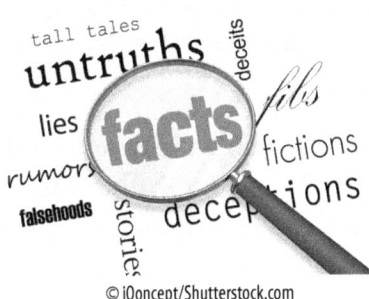

- Gun control
    - What is it?
    - Does it work?
    - What does the second amendment to the US Constitution actually mean?

Arguing Policy

When arguing policy you try to convince your audience that the scheme you have to fix something will work. Policy arguments could be about

- Requiring women to register for the Selective Service
- Raising the driving age to 21
- Legalizing drugs

You of course have to use facts to support you point, but the object here is to get people to sign on to your solution to a problem.

- Problem: men and women are not treated equally. Men have to sign up for the Selective Service at age 18 but women don't. Solution (policy change) women have to as well.
- Problem: 17–20-year-olds drive drunk. Solution: (policy change) Raise the **driving** age to 21.
- Problem: Illegal drugs are the cause of much of the crime in the United States. Solution (policy change) Legalize drugs.

Of course your policies have to be more carefully drawn than what you see above. Below are some questions and some terms you should know. These will help you design your policy and the arguments you will make for it. They can also help in designing arguments against your policy that you can then refute.

The first thing you need to do when arguing policy is to state the **problem**. Ask "What is the overriding issue you think needs to be addressed?"

Next, ask "How does the *status quo* allow for the problem and will a change in the status quo reduce the harms it creates and/or solve the problem?" This is called **inherency**.

Your policy should address the harms caused by the status quo. Ask "Are the **harms** you see significant enough to warrant attention/change?"

Then you need a plan. Ask "What is your plan for addressing the inherency—for significantly reducing or eliminating the harms you identified as resulting from the inherency?" How are you going to fix what is wrong with the status quo?

Finally you have to answer the questions "Will your plan work? Is it a reasonable and achievable solution?" This is called **solvency**.

Throw in

- **Advantages**—To your plan…
- **Disadvantages**—To your plan or to other plans…

A discussion of ***advantages*** and ***disadvantages*** works in much the same way as the confirmation and disputation sections of the classical speech outline. This gives you a chance to not only sell the positives of your plan, but also to:

- Directly dispute stated opposition to or alternatives to your plan and/or
- Inoculate your audience against opposition that may arise.

And you have successfully argued policy.

This strategy for arguing policy meshes very nicely with the classical format:

- **Introduction**—State inherency and preview argument, building credibility as you go…
- **Narrative**—Describe harms and significance, perhaps adding a true narrative to broaden your appeals.
- **Confirmation**—Introduce your plan and discuss advantages
- **Disputation**—Engage opposition (or possible opposition) to your plan
- **Conclusion**—Summarize and make a direct call to action

Here is another way of looking at policy argument. Ask these questions

- What is the problem?
- How is the current status to blame for the problem?
- What are the negative effects of the way things are?
- How significant are those problems?
- What do you think we should do about it?
- Will your plan work?
- What are some advantages and disadvantages?

Arguing Values

Values are at the core of who people are and what they believe. The term *values* can be defined in many different ways. But there are some things that all these definitions have in common. Values tell you:

- The worth of an idea, a person, an object
- How people behave
- What attitudes people hold—positive or negative—about behaviors
- A person's moral position on issues

Values are also a(n):

- Influence on an individual's behavior

- Predictor of what someone would find good, true, important, or beautiful
- The most deeply held beliefs a person has

When a value is in dispute you have a values argument. You can't successfully argue for a value unless both parties understand the value in the same way or have a standard by which the value can be judged. So stasis plays a role here as well.

One of the reasons such argumentation is difficult is that values are personal. We hold our values because:

- They meet our basic needs
- Of who we are as individuals
- Of our individual biology

There is a relationship between our values and our needs:

- We need sleep so we value it
- We need food, so we value it
- We need safety so we value it

Each of us value things at a different level. For some, risk is more important that safety. Others value work over sleep. For still others fitting in is more valued than being unique.

Societies and cultures develop values to enable people to live in relative peace and stability with one another. Group norms are established and people agree to live by those norms. Disputes arise when individuals decide to change the value system or step out of it.

Group norms are strong predictors of what we individually value. This is true whether or not you wish to be part of the group. Values like:

- Arranged marriages are better than choosing your own spouse
- Avoiding the draft is unpatriotic
- Loyalty to family trumps everything else

As individuals we value different things in relation to cultural/societal norms:

- Different views of what is beautiful
- What constitutes violence
- Likes/dislikes in food

Values govern the choices we make:

- Is a college education important?
- Should we marry or live together?
- Should I rob this bank?

Values indicate what we ought to believe and do:

- It is/is not the government's responsibility to fund my retirement
- Animals are/are not people, too
- Individuals do/do not have a right to die

Values claims make a judgment. That judgment could be:

- ❏ A social benefit: we need to keep the elderly out of poverty
- ❏ Quality: our K–12 schools provides a poor quality education
- ❏ Aesthetic merit: ANWR (Arctic National Wildlife Refuge) is beautiful

We can't talk about values unless we also talk about attitudes and beliefs. That is because our values cause us to develop attitudes about people, places, and things. Attitudes are personal to us and run the gamut from likes/dislikes to affinities/aversions.

In other words attitudes influence the judgments we make about the world. Attitudes are learned, but can also change. And naturally you bring your attitudes into the speaking situation whether you are the speaker or an audience member. Our attitudes are also influenced by our beliefs. Beliefs are judgments we make about what is true or probable, likely or unlikely.

You need to know your audience's beliefs, attitudes, and values. This is especially true if you do not have presumption.

Many of the biggest issues facing our society today are argued as fact or policy but they really are values propositions. It's important to remember this as it is difficult to find stasis if you think you are arguing to establish a fact but your audience thinks the values aspect of the argument is where it's at.

Values arguments require tact and understanding and if you are arguing to change a value you have the burden of proof.

Typical of such issues are:

- ❏ Death Penalty
    - Is it right for the government to kill people?
    - Is it good for society that criminals pay the ultimate price?

- ❏ Gun Control
    - People value safety so they should have the ability to defend themselves.
    - People are in danger when they don't know who has a gun and who doesn't.

- ❏ Illegal Immigration
    - We are a compassionate society and must grant amnesty to those here illegally.
    - We are a society that values the rule of law. Nobody who breaks the law by coming here illegally should be granted amnesty.

- ❏ Social Security
    - Our responsibility as a nation is to keep the elderly of out poverty.
    - Our responsibility as individuals is to help keep the elderly out of poverty.

One of your jobs as a speaker to is figure out what kind of argument you need to make for the specific audience to whom you are speaking. Will you argue fact, value, or policy? It's your choice. Make a good one.

CHAPTER 6

Let's NOT Argue Like This

It is not unusual to hear someone argue from a premise that sounds right, but isn't. The premise may be one that attacks a person's character or suggests that since everyone does something you should too. These arguments are called persuasive fallacies and should be avoided.

Persuasive Fallacies
- ❏ Argue from a false premise
- ❏ Change the terms of the argument
- ❏ Don't make logical sense
- ❏ Try to confuse the issue at hand
- ❏ Are unethical

They are easy to fall into and we argue from them all the time. One reason speakers resort to these fallacies is that they are lazy persuaders. It is much easier to call people names, for example, than it is to address the actual point someone makes. Here is a list and it is by no means exhaustive. But these are the fun ones. In alphabetical order then:

Ad Hominem Argument: Latin meaning "to the man" or "to the person."

- Definition: Attack the person not the argument.
- Example: "My opponent is a jerk."
- Premise: If the audience doesn't like the person then that person's argument fails.

There are several types of ad Hominem arguments:

- **Abusive:** attacks the character of the opponent. (see above)
- **Circumstantial:** "He would say that wouldn't he." You are accusing someone of holding a position because circumstances might influence others to believe the person would hold such a position.
- *Tuquoque:* "You too" arguments. This is what children do in the playground. Nah, nah, nah . . . you do it too. Another example is a parent's difficulty in arguing against smoking pot because the parent's teenager knows the parent smoked pot.
- **Guilt By Association:** You associate your opponent with something you are sure the audience will dislike in hopes that the audience will reject your opponent's position. An example would be: "My opponent has been endorsed by 'Lying Liars of America.' Do you want to vote for such a person?"

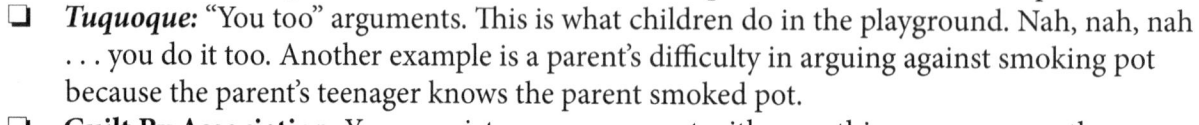

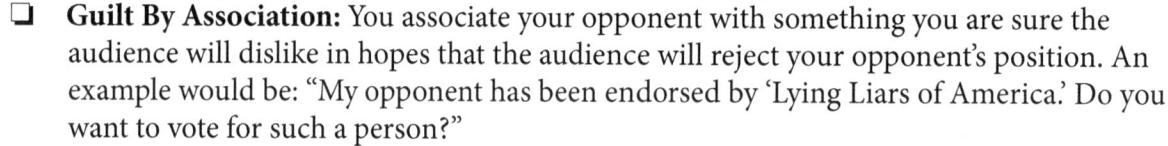

Appeal to Authority

- Definition: An argument is true because the person making it is an authority of some sort (famous, important, scholar, et al.)
- Example: Congress calls actors and actresses to testify before committees because the entertainers have made movies about issues of interest to the committee.
- Premise: Important/famous people have expertise or prestige that the audience doesn't and on that basis alone the authority should be believed.

Appeal to Ignorance (The definition of ignorance here is "lack of evidence to the contrary.")

- Definition: A claim is true because it cannot or has not yet been proven true or false.
- Example: We can believe that there is alien life on earth because we have not yet proven there isn't.
- Premise: Since my point has not been disproved you can believe it.

Appeal to Pity

- Definition: You gain acceptance of your argument by playing on emotions.
- Example: The use of starving and abused animals in Humane Society advertisements is an appeal to pity.
- Premise: People are more easily swayed by emotion than logic.

Appeal to Tradition

- Definition: We have always done it this way.
- Example: There is no need to change the two-semester college year. We have always done it this way and it works.
- Premise: The old ways are best. No argument.

Argumentum ad Populum—Latin meaning "argument of the people."

- Definition: If everyone is doing or believing it, you should too. Also called "bandwagoning."
- Example: The sun revolves around the earth. Everyone knows it's true. (It isn't of course but people used to believe that.)
- Premise: I will play on your need to fit in.

Argumentum ex Silentio: from the Latin "argument out of silence"

- Definition: Your conclusion is based on the absence of evidence.
- Examples: My opponent has never talked about whether or not she believes in Santa Claus, so she obviously does.
- Premise: You have not proved what I said isn't true.

Begging the Question

- Definition: Making your conclusion your argument.
- Example: Because assisted suicide is right and just we have to make a law that allows for assisted suicide. That is because assisted suicide is right and just.
- Premise: If I can make the audience believe the conclusion right off the bat I don't have to make an argument.

Big Lie Technique

- Definition: Repeating a lie so often that people believe it is true even though it is not. In this case you do not offer argument, you just repeat the lie.
- Example: George Washington confessed to chopping down a cherry tree. It's not true but millions of Americans believe it.
- Premise: You can make people believe something is true without evidence if you repeat that something often enough, so why bother to argue.

Cherry-Picking

- Definition: Choosing only those pieces of evidence that support your point while suppressing inconvenient facts.
- Example: Minimum wage argument. Depending on what facts are used the evidence can show that raising the minimum wage causes job loss or doesn't cause job loss. Take your pick.
- Premise: I am too much in love with my position/my position is too important to let inconvenient facts get in the way.

Chronological Snobbery

- Definition: If a bad idea was held in the past then nothing from the past is any good.
- Example: All the values held by the country in the 1950s are wrong because in the 1950s we tolerated racism and sexism.
- Premise: Nobody is redeemable.

False Dichotomy

- Definition: Your argument makes it look like there are only two choices available. You argue against one of these so the audience has no choice but to choose the one left.
- Example: You either go to college or flip burgers.
- Premise: Only present two arguments with one being obviously superior in order to manipulate the audience to get where you need to be with your argument.

Just Plain Folk

- Definition: The speaker is "just like you," an average person with the same concerns, hopes, and dreams.
- Example: Bill Clinton insisting that "I feel your pain." George H. W. Bush eating pork rinds.
- Premise: I need to build trust with my audience and this is how I am going to do it. So what if it is not true.

Loaded Words

- Definition: The use of emotionally appealing words.
- Example: "Family values" without defining what those are.
- Premise: People give meaning to words and phrases and will think you give them the same meaning if you don't define what you mean.

Moving the Goalposts

- Definition: Evidence given in response to a specific argument is deemed not enough. More is now asked for.
- Example: Sure going to college means you can make more money, but will you be happier?
- Premise: No argument in favor of a given position is ever enough.

Perfect is the Enemy of the Good

- Definition: An argument must be rejected because it is not perfect.
- Example: "If nationalized health care does not end up covering everyone it is not worth doing." Or "If the private health care market does not cover everyone then we must have national health care."
- Premise: Good is not good enough.

Poisoning the Well

- Definition: Presenting negative information about a person so as to discredit that person completely.
- Example: Suggesting that your opponent likes to view pornography in the hopes that s/he would be discredited on all issues.
- Premise: People will support me if I can make my opponent look like a bad guy.

Post Hoc ergo propter hoc—Latin "after this, therefore because of this."

- Definition: Faulty cause and effect. If this happened then it must have caused that.
- Example: We get married. We die.
- Premise: I can't figure out causation.

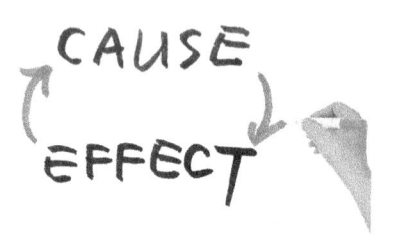

Quoting out of Context

- Definition: Giving an entirely different meaning to what someone has said by taking quotes, statistics, incidence, et al., out of context.
- Example: George Wilson, Chair of General Motors in the 1920s. His quote, "What's good for General Motors is good for the country," was taken out of context to make people believe he did not care about the country.
  - What he actually said was, "...[For] years I thought what's good for General Motors is good for the country and vice versa."
- Premise: I can make my argument and make someone look bad at the same time by quoting this person out of context.

Red Herring

- Definition: The speaker throws in a completely unrelated argument. This takes the pressure off having to defend a more difficult position.
- Example: She may have cheated on the test, but she has a stressful job.
- Premise: My arguments are not good enough. I have to distract the audience.

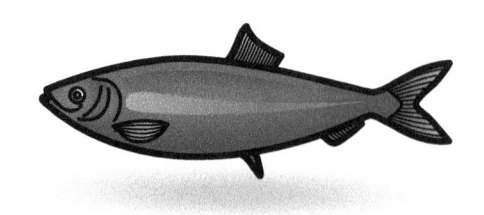

Reductio ad Absurdum

- Definition: You challenge an argument or position by reducing it to its most absurd extreme.
- Example: If we legalize marijuana everyone will be in a dope-induced haze and eating themselves silly.
- Premise: I can't win my argument unless I make people think the most absurd thing.

Reductio ad Hitlerum (Godwin's Law)

- Definition: Calling your opponent a Nazi to put him/her outside of polite society.
- Example: Hitler supported gun control (true, by the way), so if you support gun control you are a Nazi.
- Premise: I can make my opponent lose by equating her/him with Hitler.

Shifting the Burden of Proof

- Definition: Requiring your opponent to prove that what you say is not true.
- Example: It is obvious that Lizard People are trying to take over the world. Let my opponent prove it's not true.
- Premise: My position is so obviously true I should not have to prove it.

Slippery Slope

- Definition: If one domino falls they all will.
- Example: If we are forced to register our guns then it is only a matter of time before our guns will be confiscated.
- Premise: A chain of events cannot be stopped.

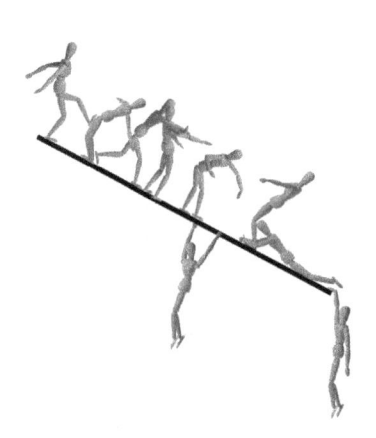

Straw man

- Definition: Your argument is based on misrepresenting your opponent's position.
- Example: Insisting that your opponent wants to reinstitute the draft because s/he believes that women should be required to sign up for the Selective Service.
- Premise: I have to hide my arguments and make it look like my opponents believe something they don't.

© 1000 words/Shutterstock.com

Run For Your Life!

Avoiding the Persuasive Fallacies

© MIgel/Shutterstock.com

Here are some questions you can ask to help you avoid falling into these and other fallacies:

- Am I insulting, demeaning, or calling my opponents names?
- Am I using "allness" language? Using words like "all," "always," "never."
- Am I attributing ideas to people that they don't have?
- Have I provided arguments for my position, not just assertions?
- What tendencies do I have when arguing? Am I likely to routinely fall into any of these fallacies?
- Am I actually arguing my point or have I introduced unnecessary side arguments?
- Am I quoting accurately and fairly when I quote people?

One Last Note

The list of persuasive fallacies in this chapter include items that can be used to make legitimate arguments. Fallacies are not fallacies everywhere and always. For example:

- We appeal to authority when we quote an expert to support a point we are making. (Appeal to Authority)
    - The key here is to make sure that the authority actually knows the subject
    - That the authority is actually correct about what s/he is saying
    - That the authority is not the only evidence you have

- We show that one thing directly leads to another and then to another (Slippery Slope) when for example we speak about regulating cigarettes. Regulating cigarettes led to
    - Banning cigarette ads which led to
    - Smoking areas in restaurants which led to
    - No smoking allowed in restaurants and bars which led to
    - No smoking in buildings in general which led to in some states
    - No smoking in your car if there are children present (beginning in October 2015 in England)

- We use 'down home' examples (Just Plain Folks) to help the audience identify with us as speakers. These can be legitimate arguments
    - As long as the examples are true and
    - Do not misrepresent us

PART TWO
The Progymnasmata

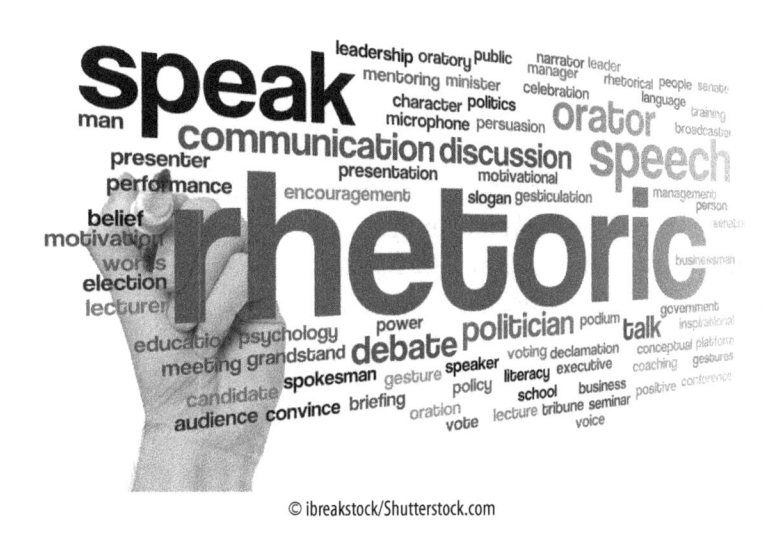

Here we are at the part where we talk about how the ancient Greeks went about teaching their students how to speak. Remember that to the ancient Greeks rhetoric was synonymous with citizenship. Learning to speak well meant learning to be a good citizen, because

- ❏ A citizen had to be able to present a case either in the assembly or in court.
- ❏ Any citizen could be called on to speak at any time.
- ❏ A citizen was expected to participate in the affairs of the city-state.

The exercises the ancient rhetoricians used taught the citizen-speaker several things:

- ❏ What constitutes supporting material for a speech
- ❏ How to develop that supporting material and arrange it appropriately
- ❏ How to compose an effective argument
- ❏ How to craft an elegant speech that is both argument and art

The Progymnasmata also incorporates the Aristotlean proofs we looked at earlier.

- ❏ The tale or narrative, chreia and proverb exercises for example are a perfect fit for pathos arguments.
- ❏ The chreia and proverb exercises could also be used to produce ethos arguments.
- ❏ The confirmation and refutation exercises can be used to produce logos arguments.

A useful exercise is to check which parts of the Progymnasmata you are using in your speech and what you are using them for. Doing so allows you to check how many ethos, pathos, and logos arguments you have made.

The first seven exercises in the Progymnasmata are:

- ❏ Fable
- ❏ Tale
- ❏ Chreia
- ❏ Proverb
- ❏ Refutation
- ❏ Confirmation
- ❏ Commonplace

Once a student had mastered these, s/he could begin composing the full speeches that make up the last seven exercises. These remaining seven exercises fit into the categories of speeches that today we call informative, persuasive, and ceremonial. The list varies depending on the ancient rhetorician but generally the final exercises look like this:

- ❏ Encomium
- ❏ Invective
- ❏ Comparison
- ❏ Description
- ❏ Character
- ❏ Thesis
- ❏ Introduction to Law

When asked to speak in a given situation you will need to decide which type of speech you will give. The occasion for the speech will usually alert you to this.

- ❏ You are at a wedding giving the toast
- ❏ You are at a political rally supporting a candidate
- ❏ You are at a business meeting presenting the latest economic forecast
- ❏ You are at a funeral delivering the eulogy
- ❏ You are introducing someone at a banquet
- ❏ You are making remarks about someone at a retirement dinner
- ❏ You are acknowledging people in an audience
- ❏ You are introducing a video
- ❏ You are encouraging people to buy a product
- ❏ You are giving a commencement speech at graduation

When you have mastered the exercises in this text you will be able to compose a speech to fit any speaking situation in which you find yourself.

CHAPTER 7

Exercise 1—Fable

© spiritofamerica/Shutterstock.com

A fable is a story usually, but not always, told through the device of talking animals, whose purpose is to present a moral. Fables are cultural artifacts, therefore, they illustrate opinions, attitudes, behaviors, and values known to and approved of or disapproved of by a society at large.

The fable is a story that conveys a meaning, generally a moral principle by which people should live. In a speech on saving for retirement you might use a fable as an example of thrift and foresight (The Grasshopper and the Ant) and then add a "human" example that amplifies the fable. Doing this "double-take" on the moral strengthens your argument that it is better to think ahead and prepare than to rely on the kindness of others.

Exercise: The fable exercise requires that a speaker choose a fable, read that fable aloud to the others assembled, and explain the moral.

Purpose: To teach the citizen-speaker how to recite someone else's story using that person's language. This teaches the new speaker important lessons.

- Using someone else's words is difficult
- You don't "sound like yourself" and therefore the recitation can sound awkward
- Many fables are translations from other languages
    - Some of these are old and use archaic words
    - Your audience may be unfamiliar with the words
    - The words may now have a very different or new inappropriate meaning
- The translation you choose may have long sentences that make for difficult recitation

Why does a speaker need to know how to tell a story? Well, story-telling is a type of argument. Stories are often used to make pathos arguments. They appeal to the values, needs, desires, and emotions of the listener. In the case of the fable, the speaker would be arguing for or against the moral the fable presents or the speaker would use the fable to prove the point about the moral.

The assumption when using a fable in a speech is that you will use it word for word as it has been translated for you. The fable is not generally paraphrased. Since this is the case here is what you need to think about.

How will I use a fable in my speech?

- As the attention-getter in an introduction
    - The fable has to relate to the speech purpose
    - The fable needs to make sense as an opening
- As an example for the point the speaker is making
- As a pathos argument

Do I memorize the fable or read it?

- Memorization allows for maximum eye contact
- Reading it gives the illusion of storytelling

Which translation should I use?

- Would an old-fashioned translation with archaic wording be the best?
- Would a modern translation be a better choice?

Do I know the meanings of all the words in the fable?

- Look up words you are not familiar with.
- Check for pronunciation.

Do I understand what is happening in the fable?

- Is the story clear to me?
- Will it be to my listeners?
- If not should I change the fable or the translation?

What do I do with the sentence structure?

- Long sentences are difficult for listeners to follow
- Break up long sentences into thought-units by the use of vocal pauses

Do I state the moral at the end of the fable?

- ❏ Your choice here
- ❏ Stating the moral makes it clear to the audience what you are trying to argue
- ❏ You have to do this if you are interpreting a fable in a unique or different way than the fable is normally understood.
    - The Three Little Pigs is usually interpreted from the pigs' point-of-view
    - Interpreting from the wolf's point of view will suggest a different moral to the story.

How dramatic should I be when I recite the fable?

- ❏ Again this is your choice
- ❏ You are telling a story. Do not read. Tell.
- ❏ You should not "act" but you should read with meaning
    - Use vocal variety
    - Use pausing, rate, and pitch

There are numerous websites devoted to fables. Go browsing. If you need some help you can practice with the following fables:

Practice Fables

The Three Fishes (A Fable from India)

Three fishes lived in a pond. It is told that one day, a fisherman passed by the pond and saw the fishes. Seeing that the pond was full of fish he decided to come back the next day to catch them.

When the wisest of the three fishes heard this, he was afraid. He spoke to the other fish and insisted that they all leave the pond. The second wisest fish agreed, but the third wisest did not. He wished to stay in the pond and trust to his luck.

The wisest of the fishes left the pond that night. The next day the second wisest fish left. The third fish laughed at the others as he swam around the pond, trusting that the fisherman would not come.

© Krasowit/Shutterstock.com

But the fisherman did come and he caught the third wisest fish in his nets.

Moral: Do not rely solely on luck.

The Lion and the Rabbit (A Fable from India)

Deep in the forest lived a lion who was killing and eating all the other animals. To save their own lives the other animals made a pact with the lion that they would send him one animal a day to eat, if he would then not kill the others. The lion agreed. Soon it was the rabbit's turn to be eaten. But the rabbit was unafraid. In fact he was even late to the lion's

© Gavran333/Shutterstock.com

den. This made the lion very angry. "You dare come late to my den?" the lion roared. "Why, yes," the rabbit explained. "You see on the way to your den I came across a mighty beast, another lion, who claimed to be the King of all the forest and he does not think much of you at all. He says you are a thief and a liar and that he is the stronger." At hearing this the lion was even more angry and demanded that the rabbit take him to the pretender. The rabbit took him to a well in the middle of the forest and told him that the other lion was hiding inside. Looking inside the well the lion saw what he thought was his rival and let out a terrible roar. The roar echoed back twice as loud fooling the lion into believing that his rival was below. He jumped into the well with the intent to do battle, but indeed met his death.

Moral: Intelligence is power.

The Ass in the Lion's Skin (An Aesop's Fable)

An ass found a lion's skin in the forest. Thinking that he could now be the most powerful beast in the forest he put on the Lion's skin and roamed about in the forest frightening the other animals. At last he came upon Mr. Fox, and tried to frighten him also. But Mr. Fox was not fooled. On hearing the ass's voice he laughed and said, "Your skin is the skin of a lion, but your voice is the voice of an ass. I would have been frightened if I had not heard your voice."

Moral: Clothes may disguise a fool, but his words will give him away.

© rook76/Shutterstock.com

Hercules and the Waggoner (An Aesop's Fable)

A Waggoner was once driving a heavy load along a very muddy road. At last the road became so muddy that the wheels of his wagon sank half-way into the mire. The more his horses pulled, the deeper the wheels sank. Throwing down his whip, the Waggoner sank to his knees and prayed to Hercules the Strong.

"O Hercules the strong, help me in this my hour of need," prayed he.

But Hercules appeared to him, and said: " Odsbods, man, don't prostrate thyself there. Get thee up and put thy shoulder to the wheel."

© Vladimir Korostyshevskiy/Shutterstock.com

Moral: The gods help them that help themselves.

The Crow and the Pitcher (An Aesop's Fable)

A Crow, half-dead with thirst, came upon a Pitcher which had once been full of water; but when the Crow put its beak into the mouth of the Pitcher he found that only very little water was left in it, and that he could not reach far enough down to get at it. He tried, and he tried, but at last had to give up in despair. Then a thought came to him, and he took a pebble and dropped it into the Pitcher. Then he took another pebble and dropped it into the Pitcher. Then he took another pebble and dropped that into the Pitcher. Then he took another pebble and dropped that into the Pitcher. Then he took another pebble and dropped that into the Pitcher. Then he took another pebble and dropped that into the Pitcher. At last, at last, he saw the water mount up near him, and after casting in a few more pebbles he was able to quench his thirst and save his life.

Moral: Little by little does the trick.

The Boy Who Cried Wolf (An Aesop's Fable)

There was once a young Shepherd Boy who tended his sheep at the foot of a mountain near a dark forest. It was rather lonely for him all day, so he thought upon a plan by which he could get a little company and some excitement. He rushed down towards the village calling out "Wolf, Wolf," and the villagers came out to meet him, and some of them stopped with him for a considerable time. This pleased the boy so much that a few days afterwards he tried the same trick, and again the villagers came to his help. But shortly after this a Wolf actually did come out from the forest, and began to worry the sheep, and the boy of course cried out "Wolf, Wolf," still louder than before. But this time the villagers, who had been fooled twice before, thought the boy was again deceiving them, and nobody stirred to come to his help. So the Wolf made a good meal off the boy's flock, and when the boy complained, the wise man of the village said:

Moral: "Nobody believes a liar ... even when he is telling the truth!"

The Two Wolves (Cherokee Fable)

One evening an old Cherokee, sitting by the fire, told his grandson about a great battle that goes on inside all people. "My son," he said, "the battle that goes on inside us is between two 'wolves' that live in all of us."

The one is called Evil. He is the spirit of sorrow, greed, guilt, lust, envy, jealousy, regret, arrogance, self-pity, resentment, inferiority, lies, and pride.

The other is called Good. He is the spirit of hope, peace, humility, kindness, contentment, joy, generosity, truth, compassion and faith.

The grandson sat in thought for many minutes. He then lifted his head and asked, "Inside us. Who wins?"

The grandfather replied, "The one you feed."

Moral: You will become what you spend the most time on.

The Farmer's Horse and His Dog (A Russian fable)

A dog and a Horse, who both belonged to the same farmer, began, one day, to dispute as to which had given the more valuable services.

"You have done nothing to boast of!" said the Dog, "I shouldn't be surprised to see you driven off the farm altogether! A noble career, indeed, to slave all day dragging a plow or a cart. Yet I never heard of your doing anything finer! How can you possibly think yourself my equal? I never rest day or night. All day long I watch the cattle in the meadow; and throughout the night I guard the house."

"I don't deny it," replied the Horse, "All that you say is quite true. Only, please remember that if it were not for my plow there would be nothing at all for you to guard."

Moral: Everyone's job is important.

The Lion and the Cows (A fable from Afghanistan)

In a meadow, a brown, a black, and a white cow lived happily together.

One day a lion came to the meadow and saw the cows. He thought, "This is fine. I can stay and prey on the cows. They will provide my food for a long time."

The next day he attacked one of the cows but the other two defended their friend and during the battle the Lion was injured and was forced to retreat.

The lion thought carefully about what had happened and decided that he could not win his prey if the cows stayed together. So he devised a plan.

The next day the Lion came back to the meadow. He went to the cows and shouted, "I am sorry for the misunderstanding yesterday. I like this place and would like to stay. If you let me I will protect you from your enemies."

The cows thought about this and agreed to let the lion stay.

So the Lion stayed there for some days. One day he saw that the White cow was far away from the others. He convinces the Brown and Black cow that the White cow would eat them out of house and home.

Fearful of starving the two cows agreed that the Lion could kill their friend and so the Lion did.

Then another day he saw that the two were eating far apart.

He came to the Brown cow and convinced that Brown cow that he and the lion had so much in common that they should band together against the Black cow. The Brown cow agreed and the Lion killed the Black cow. Finally that Lion became hungry again.

He came to the Brown cow and said, "While we are best friends, I am hungry. I must kill you and eat you."

The Brown cow knew that as with the White cow and the Black that alone he had no defense against the Lion, so he accepted his fate.

Moral: Self-interest leads to a bad end.

CHAPTER 8

Exercise 2—Tale or Narrative

In the traditional Progymnasmata the tale exercise was designed to help the citizen-speaker paraphrase a narrative. This exercise fits neatly into the second part of the classical pattern of organization, the narratio or "laying out the case." As is true with the fable, the tale allows you to use a pathos argument, but can also be used as an ethos argument. It does this by building the credibility of the speaker who has chosen the tale and by the content of the tale itself. The difference between the fable and the tale is:

- Fables are generally shorter and present a moral. They usually use anthropomorphized animals as characters.
- Tales can be about anything. They do not have to present a moral. They may require paraphrase to work effectively.

The tale or narrative is an important rhetorical tool. You can see the truth of this as you read newspaper or news blog stories. These stories give a human face to cold facts. Tales add in helping the audience identify with the speaker, the topic, and the persuasive intent of the speech.

A tale or a narrative can be composed of one event or many. Your choice in this regard will be based on your assessment of your audience, your specific speech purpose, and your choice of arguments.

Exercise: Chose a tale or narrative and tell the story in your own words. Any tale or narrative could work for this exercise.

Purpose: To teach the following:

- How to distinguish important elements in the story from the unimportant.
- How to tell a story in a way that supports your argument while being ethical about its meaning.
- Paraphasing
- How to use examples (tales) as argument.

The paraphrase or retelling of the tale also solves several of the problems encountered in the fable exercise.

- You are using your own words so you sound like you.
- You can change archaic words and phrases to more modern usage.
- You can change sentence structure, length, and cadence so the tale is now oral rather than written in style.

What tale should I choose?

- You can use tales that already exist. If you do you will simply paraphrase the tale.
- You can take a tale and reverse the point-of-view. Disney has done this with the movie *Maleficent*—a retelling of *The Sleeping Beauty* from Maleficent's point of view.
- You can look at this exercise as a type of fan fiction. Fan fiction takes elements from published works and uses them to further a story or a universe. Popular fan fiction includes new stories based on the *Lord of the Rings*, *Harry Potter,* or *Hunger Games*. This is, in effect, what screenwriters do when they add to or subtract from a story so the story works for film.
    - Disney animated movies diverge wildly (in some cases) from the original fairy tales.
- You can make up your own tales. You might take an existing tale (think of any fairy tale) and imitate it. Or you might think about those elements that exist in most tales and compose one that is entirely your own.
- You might tell a story from your own life. This is an effective use of tale as you know the story well. And you have told it many times so you have practice at it.

Practice Tale

Snow White

You probably think you know this tale as you are acquainted with the Disney version of the story or have seen either or both of the 2012 movie adaptations **Snow White and the Huntsman** and **Mirror, Mirror**. These are the most recent telling of this tale but people have been retelling this tale since the first play based on the story produced in 1912. The interesting thing is that most of these adaptations are not very much like the original in some important ways. Below you will find an outline of the original story and then we will talk about how the story has been adapted for different audiences. Have fun.

© Marco Brockmann/Shutterstock.com

Snow White and the Seven Dwarfs as told by the Brothers Grimm

Rather than tell the entire tale here we will list the basic elements of the story.

- ❏ The story begins with a queen wishing for a daughter who was "as white as snow, as red as blood, as black as ebony."
- ❏ The king and queen have a daughter they name Snow White. She has skin as white as snow, lips as red as blood, and hair as black as ebony.
- ❏ The queen dies.
- ❏ The king remarries a beautiful but vain woman who wants to be the most beautiful in the land.
- ❏ The Queen has a magic mirror. The mirror talks to her and can only speak the truth. Their conversations generally include: "Mirror, mirror on the wall, who is the fairest of them all?" The mirror would reply, "You are the fairest, lady Queen."
- ❏ Snow White grows up.
- ❏ The queen asks her daily question and this time the mirror answers that Snow White is the fairest.
- ❏ The queen decides to kill Snow White. She calls a huntsman to her and tells him to take her into the forest and remove her lungs and her liver and bring them back as proof that she is dead. The huntsman obeys but at the last cannot bring himself to kill Snow White.
- ❏ He finds and kills a wild boar and brings back its lungs and liver and took those to the queen, which the queen subsequently eats for dinner.
- ❏ Snow White runs off into the forest.
- ❏ Deep in the forest she finds a cottage all shiny and clean inside.
- ❏ It has seven of everything inside. And everything is small. Snow White eats some food and then falls asleep on one of the seven little beds in the cottage.
- ❏ The cottage belongs to seven dwarfs who mine for ore all day.
- ❏ They find her asleep when they come home from work. When she wakes up in the morning they strike a bargain. She will take care of their cottage and they will protect her from the wicked queen. Snow White agrees, and so she begins living with the Seven Dwarfs in their cottage in the forest.
- ❏ Naturally the queen finds out Snow White is not dead. That pesky mirror always tells the truth.

- So the queen makes three attempts to kill her through magic.
    - She disguises herself as a peddler and sells Snow White some ribbons with which to lace up Snow White's corset. Snow White buys the ribbons, has her corset laced up and falls down as if dead. The dwarfs come and rescue her.
    - The queen then tries the same trick with a poisoned comb for Snow White's hair. As soon as Snow White puts the comb in her hair she falls down as if dead. The dwarfs come and rescue her.
    - Finally the queen comes with the apple. Snow White eats it and falls down as if dead. This time the dwarfs cannot revive her.
- The dwarfs build a glass casket for her and they put her in the forest and go to mourn her every day.
- Finally a prince rides by. He sees her and falls in love with her.
- The dwarfs agree to let the prince take the casket away with him.
- As his men are carrying the casket they stumble and jostle it. The piece of poisoned apple is dislodged from Snow White's throat. She wakes up.
- The prince and Snow White decide to marry. A great wedding feast is planned and everyone is invited.
- The Queen discovers that the new bride whose wedding she has been invited to is now the fairest in the land because naturally the mirror has told her.
- The queen goes to the wedding to see for herself this fairest of brides and is astonished to discover that the bride is Snow White.
- During the feast a pair of red hot iron shoes are given to the queen and she is forced to put them on and dance until she falls down dead.

Now let's look at what has been done to this story over the years.

The Disney Version

Snow White and the Seven Dwarfs (1937)

Here are the changes:

- ❏ The movie begins with a prologue.
- ❏ At the beginning of the film both of Snow White's parents are dead.
- ❏ Snow White is a teenager.
- ❏ The prince is introduced early in the story.
- ❏ The dwarfs are given names.
- ❏ The huntsman brings back the heart of a wild boar to prove that Snow White is dead.
- ❏ The dwarfs' cottage is a mess and Snow White cleans it before they get home.
- ❏ The queen comes only once to the cottage to try to kill Snow White.
- ❏ The device she uses is a poisoned apple.
- ❏ The dwarfs chase the queen through the forest and she falls to her death from a cliff.
- ❏ The prince finds Snow White in the glass casket. He kisses her and this is what awakens her.
- ❏ They live happily ever after.

What you see here is that Disney has made the story less graphic and violent. The huntsman takes a heart and not the lungs and liver from the wild boar. The queen does not eat the heart. The ending is changed so the queen is responsible for her own death and does not die from what looks very much like torture. Remember, this adaptation was for 20th century children, so naturally the more violent parts of the story are omitted.

The story has also been streamlined. Fairy Tales often place elements in groups of three. So in the original story the queen goes three times to the cottage to try to kill Snow White. But that doesn't work for a movie. The Disney version retains the poisoned apple but eliminates the other two magical killing devices.

Other changes in the story include: the early introduction of the prince; love's first kiss as the way Snow White is revived; the dwarfs have names.

The changes made to this story in its various adaptations are made to appeal to specific audiences and to make thematic changes or persuasive points. For example, in **Snow White and the Huntsman (2012):**

- ❏ Snow White is older, she does not find the dwarfs in a house nor is she a housekeeper for them. She becomes the head of an army. The huntsman may or may not be a love interest for her.
- ❏ The queen has a name, a brother, and a back story.
- ❏ The dwarfs are comical but real.
- ❏ The poisoned apple is used, but the love's first kiss is not what you would expect.

All of this was done to appeal to the same audience that likes *Twilight* and *The Hunger Games*. The way the story is told is meant to be persuasive for this specific audience.

***Mirror Mirror* (2012)** is in some ways a more interesting adaptation as it completely eliminates the beauty aspect of the queen's obsession and replaces it with money. In this telling of the tale:

- ❏ The queen uses the mirror to wreak havoc on her enemies.
- ❏ Snow White is *persona non grata* because she is in love with someone the queen wishes to marry for his money.
- ❏ The dwarfs live in the forest but apparently make their living robbing people traveling through it.
- ❏ Snow White kisses the prince to break a spell that has been cast on him.
- ❏ There is no huntsman.
- ❏ Snow White's father turns out not to be dead but under enchantment.
- ❏ The evil queen does eventually try the apple trick but is thwarted at the end.

One thing to notice about all these adaptations is that while they are very different from one another, as they are pitched to different audiences, they all contain a few elements that tell you they are the same story.

- ❏ An evil stepmother queen
- ❏ Supposedly or actually dead parents
- ❏ A beautiful young Snow White
- ❏ A dangerous forest
- ❏ Dwarfs
- ❏ A poisoned apple
- ❏ A prince

The essence of the story is still there, the telling of it is because the audience and culture have changed.

CHAPTER 9

Exercise 3—Chreia

> DOGS KEEP
> A PROMISE
> A PERSON CAN'T.
>
> HANNIBAL[1]

© Yury Zap/Shutterstock.com

The chreia exercise is a sister exercise to the proverb and is sometimes called the Anecdote Exercise. The *chreia's* subject is a saying or deed by a person the speaker admires. The exercise requires the citizen-speaker to illustrate a virtue or teach a moral lesson. It has the added advantage of teaching the citizen-speaker how to begin to construct ethos arguments using the saying or deed.

Exercise: The citizen-speaker analyzes a saying or deed by a famous or important person with the twin goals of using that person as an authority and amplifying a virtue. The chreia could include:

- ❏ An important action this person performed
- ❏ An important or pithy saying of the person
- ❏ Or both

Purpose: To learn how to make ethos arguments. Ethos arguments are arguments based on the credibility of the source. The idea is that if a person who is acknowledged as an authority or is in some other way important or famous thinks, believes, or does something important, learned or otherwise credible, then the audience can feel comfortable thinking, believing, or doing it too. These can also be used to make pathos arguments, as in arguing a value or virtue. Many stories about people are told to emphasize a virtue the person holds and to encourage the audience to become virtuous like the person selected for the *chreia*.

To do this exercise as the ancient Greeks did you would do the following:

- ❏ Choose a saying or action of a famous person
- ❏ Praise the saying or deed and the author of the saying or deed
- ❏ Restate the saying or deed in a way that is understandable to the audience
- ❏ Tell a story that illustrates the meaning of the saying or deed
- ❏ Tell a story that is a contrast or opposite to the saying or the deed
- ❏ Give an example by analogy. How is this saying or deed similar to something else the audience can identify with?
- ❏ Give an example
- ❏ Give testimony by others in support of your point
- ❏ Conclude

This can be a long exercise if you do all of the steps above. The ancient rhetorician thought it important to learn how to, what they called, "amplify" a subject. Taking a simple saying or deed and speaking about it for many minutes was a talent they prized.

For modern day speakers this extensive amplification may not be necessary, but the basic exercise can be helpful. For us the following will make a very acceptable *chreia* and teach the same basic lessons.

- ❏ Choose a saying or deed of a famous person
- ❏ Praise the author of the saying or deed
- ❏ Praise the saying or deed as something admirable
- ❏ Tell a story that illustrates the saying or deed
- ❏ Give an example or tell a story that contrasts with the saying or deed
- ❏ Give testimony in support of the saying or deed
- ❏ Conclude

Suggested Quotes for the Chreia Exercise

I am so fast that last night I turned off the light in my hotel room and was in bed before the room was dark.—Muhammad Ali

Everything we hear is an opinion, not a fact. Everything we see is a perspective, not a truth.—Marcus Aurelius

A large income is the best recipe for happiness I have ever heard of.—Jane Austen

All action results from thoughts, so it is thoughts that matter.—Sai Baba

Housework can't kill you, but why take the chance?—Phyllis Diller

People seldom do what they believe in. They do what is convenient and then repent.—Bob Dylan

A good nation I will make live.—Black Elk

First learn the meaning of what you say, then speak.—Epictetus

There is nothing impossible to him who will try.—Alexander the Great

I like criticism. It makes you strong.—LeBron James

One of the disadvantages of wine is that it makes a man mistake words for thoughts.—Samuel Johnson

I can accept failure. Everyone fails at something. But I can't accept not trying.—Michael Jordan

I saw the angel in the marble and carved until I set him free.—Michelangelo

The time is always right to do what is right.—Martin Luther King, Jr.

For every complex problem there is an answer that is clear, simple and wrong.—H. L. Mencken

In a time of universal deceit—telling the truth is a revolutionary act.—George Orwell

Let us not pray to be sheltered from dangers but to be fearless when facing them.— Rabindranath Tagore

Age is an issue of mind over matter. If you don't mind, it doesn't matter.—Mark Twain

Between two evils I always pick the one I haven't tried before.—Mae West

Lots of people want to ride with you in the limo, but what you want is someone who will take the bus with you when the limo breaks down.—Oprah Winfrey

If you don't have time to do it right, when will you have the time to do it over?—John Wooden

Sample Chreia Pairs

The most difficult part of the Chreia exercise is finding a counter quote. As the Chreia exercise begins the process of learning how to argue against an opponent's position, it is important to find a credible source that voices the opposing point of view. Here are some examples of quote/counter quote.

No one in the 'verse can stop me—River Tam

A man's got to know his limitations—Dirty Harry Callahan

A government of laws not of men—John Adams

Show me the man and I will find you the crime—Laurentiy Beria

He who has a why can live any how.—Friedrich Nietzche

Tomorrow, and tomorrow, and tomorrow,
Creeps in this petty pace from day to day,
To the last syllable of recorded time;
And all our yesterdays have lighted fools
The way to dusty death. Out, out, brief candle!
Life's but a walking shadow, a poor player,
That struts and frets his hour upon the stage,
And then is heard no more. It is a tale
Told by an idiot, full of sound and fury,
Signifying nothing.—Macbeth/Shakespeare

All this self-sacrifice is a sad mistake—Gertrude Rhead

A hero is someone who has given his or her life to something bigger than oneself
—Joseph Campbell

Example Chreia

Here is an example of using a chreia and amplifying it.

Saying: Well, I'm what I am and I'm what I'm not; I'm sure happy with what I've got. I live to love and laugh a lot, and that's all I need.—*Kenny Chesney, "Never Wanted Nothing More"*

- *Praise for the Author*—Kenny Chesney is a well-known American Country music artist. Kenny Chesney's songs are often reflections on his own life, yet they resonate meaning on a general level. Chesney's lyrics are nostalgic and reflect on the joy of life's simple pleasures.

- *Paraphrase of Saying*—It is important to live your life to the fullest through love and laughter. You should find happiness in being yourself, and not through material gain or envy of others.

- *Causes or Reasons for Saying*—Many people try to be someone else because they are envious. There are others that are greedy and wish to obtain material possessions. It is important to be yourself and be happy with what you have been given. It is also important to love and to laugh and to find joy in life and to remember that you are blessed to have what you do because there is always someone less fortunate than you.

- *A Contrast*—"Someday I want to be rich. Some people get so rich they lose all respect for humanity. That's how rich I want to be."—Rita Rudner
    - There are many people who may only be happy if they 'have' everything that they want in life. Their need to gain often overshadows their ability to see life for what it should be. They may not be able to find joy in the simple pleasures of life because they are consumed with their greed.

- *A Comparison*—"It's funny how it's the little things in life that mean the most—not where you live, what you drive, or the price tag on your clothes. There is no dollar sign on a piece of mind, this I've come to know."—*Zac Brown Band, 'Chicken Fried'*

- This song also discusses the appreciation one should have for their lives without having to place a price on happiness.

- *An Example*—I recently had the opportunity to interview my Grandmother for a course on The Perspectives on Aging. Though I am very close with my Grandmother (and have been my entire life) she never really went in to detail about her life. My Grandmother grew up on a farm, with very little money. She then went on to raise six children while my Grandfather worked to support them. Money was never an issue for my Grandparents, simply because they didn't have any. They got by on what they had and spent every moment they could with their children. My Grandparents instilled these values into their own children. When asked if my Grandmother would change anything about her life, she simply replied "No, I am lucky to have had the life I did and the family that I have."

- *Epilogue*—Though I do not often take advice from the lyrics of a song, I believe that this particular line in Kenny Chesney's *'Never Wanted Nothing More'* is a prime example of words that one should live by. ("Chreia" 2011)

CHAPTER 10

Exercise 4—Proverb

> AN **APPLE A DAY** KEEPS THE **DOCTOR AWAY**

© Archiwiz/Shutterstock.com

This exercise requires the citizen-speaker to use proverbs to support a point. Proverbs are pithy sayings known to the culture at large that reveal a truth about life that the culture understands to be true. Proverbs were seen as holding truth so they could be used to argue a point. Proverbs were, in fact, considered persuasive in and of themselves.

Exercise: This exercise is similar to the chreia. The difference between the two is that the proverb exercise amplifies a moral truth or right behavior using a saying **not** attributed to a person.

Purpose: The exercise teaches the citizen-speaker how to use testimony as a persuasive tool. Proverbs can be used to make both ethos and pathos arguments.

In the ancient Greek world opinion was valued as argument because opinion resided in the community and not the individual. That is why proverbs worked as argument for them and similarly can work for us today. As long as the culture, or at least your audience, subscribes to the basic ideas presented in the proverb the argument holds.

Originally the exercise required these eight parts:

- ❏ Praise the proverb as having something important to say
- ❏ Paraphrase the proverb to make sure everyone knows what it means
- ❏ Explain why the meaning of the proverb is important
- ❏ Compare the proverb to something else
- ❏ Use testimony to support the meaning of the proverb
- ❏ Give an example of the benefits of following the proverb
- ❏ Contrast the meaning with something worse
- ❏ Conclude

For our purposes this exercise requires:

- ❏ Open with the proverb
- ❏ Explain what the proverb means and why one should follow its advice
- ❏ Contrast the proverb with its opposite
- ❏ Give an example or a quote to support the proverb
- ❏ Conclude

Here are some proverbs from around the world. If the proverb is not from your culture you may wish to find one that says the same thing that is, unless you wish to study that culture to make sure you can reasonably understand and use the proverb.

Proverbs for Practice

There is not enough room for two elephants to sit in the shade.—Angola

To be willing is only half the task.—Armenia

Other people's eggs have two yolks.—Bulgaria

If you are patient in one moment of anger, you will escape a hundred days of sorrow.—Chinese

When a bee comes to your house let her have beer; you may want to visit her house someday.—Congo

Do not protect yourself by a face, but rather by your friends.—Czech Republic

He who is afraid of asking is afraid of learning.—Denmark

The town is new every day.—Estonia

He who conceals his disease can expect to be cured.—Ethiopia

There is no eel so small but it hopes to become a whale.—German

If things are getting easier maybe you are headed downhill.—Ghana

When a camel is at the foot of a mountain, then judge of his height.—Hindu

Better one good thing that is than two good things that were.—Ireland

Teeth placed before the tongue give good advice.—Italy

Fall seven times. Stand up eight.—Japan

Don't think there are no crocodiles because the water is still.—Malaysia

If you wish good advice consult an old man.—Rumania

A man without a wife is like a man in winter without a fur hat.—Russia

The absent are always at fault.—Spain

Go often to the house of a friend; for weeds soon choke up the unused path.—Sweden

Measure a thousand times, cut once.—Turkey

Man has responsibility, not power.—Tuscarora Nation (Native American)

Hope Spring eternal.—United States

More Practice Proverbs Commonly Used in the United States

Haste makes waste.

A stitch in time saves nine.

Look before you leap.

The squeaky wheel gets the grease.

An apple a day keeps the doctor away.

Mother knows best.

A bird in the hand is worth two in the bush.

Don't miss the forest for the trees.

Money can't buy happiness.

Beauty is only skin deep.

Never let the right hand know what the left is doing.

Absence makes the heart grow fonder.

Clothes make the man (or woman).

Sample Proverb Amplification

Proverb: He who hesitates is lost.

- **Praise the proverb as having something important to say.**
  - It is important to seize the day (carpe diem) or take the bull by the horns or make a decision and run with it for in this way you show a commendable courage and sense of adventure.

- **Paraphrase the proverb to make sure everyone knows what it means.**
  - This proverb tells us that we must take the opportunity that is put in front of us and not think too long and hard about it or else that opportunity might disappear.

- **Explain why the meaning of the proverb is important.**
  - Think of those times in your life when you hesitated about doing something and then life passed you by. You regretted not going on that spontaneous trip. You regretted not helping that person who needed it at the time and now you feel bad about yourself. This proverb is important to remember as it can help us avoid these regrets and feeling of having let ourselves and others down.

- **Compare the proverb to something else.**
  - This proverb is like the Latin saying "carpe diem"—seize the day.

- **Use testimony to support the meaning of the proverb.**
  - John B. Gough a prominent Temperance advocate of the 19th century said: "If you want to succeed in the world you must make your own opportunities as you go on. The man who waits for some seventh wave to toss him on dry land will find that the seventh wave is a long time a coming. You can commit no greater folly than to sit by the roadside until someone comes along and invites you to ride with him to wealth or influence."

- **Give an example of the benefits of following the proverb.**
  - It saves lives: Julie Corson, age fifteen, hopped on the school bus, took a seat up front and stared out of the window, while about twenty other kids chattered and listened to MP3s. But then, less than a mile from Newark Valley High School in upstate New York, the morning of March 6, the bus started swerving. No one knew it then, but Ed Card, the sixty-nine-year-old driver, had suffered a heart attack. "He was going off the road—we were hitting mailboxes," Corson says. Worse still, the bus was careering straight for the side of a mattress store. Now cries of fear filled the bus—and the coolheaded Corson went to work. "I got on my hands and knees and moved Mr. Card's foot off the gas," she recalls. "Then I pushed my hands on the brake." (Jerome et al. 10 02, 2006)

- **Contrast the meaning with something worse.**
  - Passing on opportunities can mean loss of income, low self-esteem, and lost love or in the case of the example above, injury or death.

- **Conclude**
  - Do not hesitate. Jump in and make a difference.

CHAPTER 11

Exercises 5 and 6— Refutation/Confirmation

Aristotle believed that all rhetoric is inherently persuasive. This belief is embedded in the Progymnasmata. We can see it in the Chreia and Proverb exercises. Notice that in both of these exercises the citizen-speaker is required to present a counter argument to the beliefs, attitudes, values, or behaviors supported or rejected by the proverb.

The Chriea and the Proverb Exercises set the citizen-speaker up for the next two exercises—the Refutation and the Confirmation—which require the citizen-speaker to choose a topic, choose a side and

- ❏ Argue against your chosen side in the **Refutation**
- ❏ Argue for your chosen side in the **Confirmation**

By requiring the citizen-speaker to present an opposing view these two exercises help the citizen-speaker learn the following lessons:

- There are legitimate arguments for and against what is being proposed
- Speakers need to anticipate audience objections to what the speaker proposes
  - Audiences will supply these arguments for themselves. Even good listeners will "argue with the speaker" in their heads

The exercises are in this order to force you to argue against your position first. This is difficult. You already know the arguments in favor of position. Finding an effective argument that refutes your position is more challenging.

Rise to the challenge. Being an effective citizen-speaker relies on it. You have to choose those arguments that best support an opponent's position and argue against them. If audience members wish to object to what you are proposing one of the easiest ways for them to do that is to say, "Well the speaker is not being fair to the other side. There are plenty of good arguments against this proposition." Being able to refute good arguments takes this objection away from the audience. It also shows that you respect your opponents and have seriously considered your opponents' arguments.

Exercise: The refutation exercise taught the citizen-speaker how to attack the credibility of a myth or legend. The confirmation exercise defended the credibility of a myth or legend.

Purpose: The refutation exercise was designed to show the citizen-speaker the many ways one could attack an opponent's arguments. It taught the citizen-speaker to learn the best approach to highlighting the weaknesses in an opponent's position. The confirmation exercise was designed to show the many ways one could present an argument in favor of a position one holds. In this way the citizen-speaker learned the best approach to showing the strength of his/her position.

The Refutation

Following the instructions of both Aphthonius and Hermogenes, two great exponents of the Progymnasmata, we can construct an outline of how to refute an opponent's position.

- State the false assertion of the opponent
- Narrative: explain the situation
- Refutation: Attack the opponent's position

The attack on the opponent's position can take many forms. A few are listed below:

- **Uncertainty**—in refuting support for the death penalty this argument would suggest that we cannot know for certain whether or not innocent people have been executed.
- **Incredibility**—in refuting an argument to lower the drinking age to eighteen this argument would suggest that it is incredible to believe that young people are capable of making good drinking/driving decisions.
- **Impossibility**—in refuting support for euthanasia this argument suggests that it is impossible to bring back to life someone who was allowed to die if it turns out that person would have recovered.

- **Lack of Consistency**—in refuting the position in favor of property taxes as the funding mechanism for public schools this argument says that property taxes create inconsistency in the amount of money schools have. (The consistency argument is often used to accuse politicians of flip-flopping on issues.)
- **Illogic**—in refuting the position that marriage is bad for you because all married people die, this argument suggests that since there is no causation between marriage and death this argument is illogical.
- **Unfitting**—in refuting the position that an incumbent senator should be reelected, this argument suggests that it is unfitting to accuse the senator's opponent of having a sense of entitlement to the senate seat because s/he served in the military.

These are types of arguments you can make. And you certainly don't have to nor should you make all of them in one speech. While these are not the only ways to argue against a position, they give you some idea of how you can frame your arguments.

The most effective way to develop the Refutation and Confirmation Exercises is to

- Choose a topic
- State that topic in the form of a question
- State your position on the topic
- Compose the Refutation speech by choosing one or two arguments that oppose your position
  - Use the most effective arguments you can find
  - Use the list on this page to help you

Our example exercise will answer this question: **Are eReaders better than books?** The position we will take for purposes of the exercise is "No. Books are better than eReaders."

Having said that, what is it we will argue in the Refutation Exercise? That's right: "Contrary to what people may think eReaders are better than books."

Example Refutation

© Bruno D'Andrea/Shutterstock.com

© Timofeyev Alexander/Shutterstock.com

The position to be attacked: Books are better than eReaders

Narrative: Technology can be a wonderful thing. We can now withdraw money from the bank at anytime. We can research papers from the comfort of our homes. We can talk, text, Instagram, Tweet, and Tumblr anytime, anywhere. But not all tech innovations are good or beneficial. One of those not so great innovations is the eReader.

eReaders are essentially electronic books. You know what they are. You probably have one. Kindle, Nook, ipads, tablets, even smart phones can be used as electronic books. But do you really want to do that? Do you really want to read from a sterile, utilitarian device? Wouldn't you rather hold in your hand a real live book of paper and ink? I would. Books are so much better than eReaders for reasons too many to count.

Not everyone thinks so, though. Why is that? Well there are *some* reasons why some may prefer eReaders:

- With an eReader you have an entire library at your fingertips.
  - You will no longer have to carry heavy books wherever you go
  - You don't have to worry about forgetting the books you need/want
- eReaders take up less space.
  - No need to have lots of shelves to house your books
  - Frees up space in your dormroom
- eReaders can be backlit so you can read in the dark without disturbing others.
- eBooks are generally less expensive than hard copy books.
- eReaders allow you to instantly look up information like definitions.

Conclusion: While I prefer hard copy books you can see that there are good reasons why someone might wish to own and use an eReader.

If this were a full-blown speech this is how you would go about attacking these arguments.

- Incredibility: it is incredible to believe that one needs an entire library at one's fingertips all day every day.
- Uncertainty: You do not know if space-saving is as beneficial as having those hard copy books physically in your house or apartment.
- Illogic: Supporters of eReaders talk as if there is no other way to read at night without disturbing others. Not only does that not make sense, it isn't true.
- Uncertainty: While some eBooks are less expensive than hard copy this is by no means true of all.
- Incredibility: It is incredible to believe that clicking on and off links while trying to read a novel or textbook will not be a distraction and cause lack of comprehension.

This of course is not as far as you would have to go in constructing arguments. You have to actually make the argument by presenting evidence to show that what you are asserting is true. For example, you would have to show by citing studies that the links in an eBook are in fact distracting to the reader.

So that's the Refutation speech.

Confirmation Exercise

So here we are, the flip side of the Refutation exercise. Here you would argue **for** a proposition. You state what you believe and prove it. If you were following the dictates of the ancient rhetoricians you would argue for the credibility of a myth or legend.

Exercise: Defend the credibility of a myth or legend.

Purpose: This exercise was designed to show the citizen-speaker the many ways one could present an argument in favor of a position the speaker holds. In this way the citizen-speaker learned the best approach to showing the strength of his/her position.

Combine this exercise with the Refutation exercise and presto! you have the **Thesis Exercise,** which we will discuss later.

This is what you have to do to compose a Confirmation exercise:

- ❏ Assert what is to be Confirmed (Tell us what you support)
- ❏ Narrative: explain the situation
- ❏ Confirmation: defend the position

The defense of your position can take many forms. A few are listed below.

- ❏ **Certainty**—in supporting the death penalty this argument would suggest that we can know for certain that those put to death will never again be able to harm another.
- ❏ **Credibility**—in supporting an argument to lower the drinking age to eighteen, this argument would suggest that it is credible to believe that young people are capable of making good drinking/driving decisions.
- ❏ **Possibility**—in supporting euthanasia, this argument suggests that it is possible to make unbiased and free decisions to end a life.
- ❏ **Consistency**—in supporting property taxes as the funding mechanism for public schools, this argument says that property taxes are consistent with constitutional protections.
- ❏ **Logic**—in supporting the idea that marriage promotes good health, this argument suggests that there is a causation between marriage and good health outcomes.
- ❏ **Fitting**—in supporting the position that an incumbent senator should be re-elected, this argument suggests that it is fitting to call into question the motives of his/her opponent.

The above arguments are suggestions. And you certainly don't have to nor can you make all of them in one speech. These are not the only ways to argue against a position, but they give you some idea of how you can frame your arguments.

And remember this is not as far as you have to go. You have to use supporting material to prove the assertion you make. For example, what studies exist and what do they say about the causal relationship between marriage and good health? You need to pick the best studies and talk about them to complete your argument.

Example Confirmation

© Bruno D'Andrea/Shutterstock.com.   © Timofeyev Alexander/Shutterstock.com

The position to be supported: Books are better than eReaders

Narrative: Technology can be a wonderful thing. We can now withdraw money from the bank at anytime. We can research papers from the comfort of our homes. We can talk, text, Instagram, Tweet, and Tumblr anytime, anywhere. But not all tech innovations are good or beneficial. One of those not so great innovations is the eReader.

eReaders are essentially electronic books. You know what they are. You probably have one. Kindle, Nook, ipads, tablets, even smart phones can be used as electronic books. But do you really want to do that? Do you really want to read from a sterile, utilitarian device? Wouldn't you rather hold in your hand a real live book of paper and ink? I would. Books are so much better than eReaders for reasons too many to count.

- People comprehend less information when reading on an eReader
- Hard copy books allow for easily reading ahead or going back and re-reading
- Books have an aesthetic appeal eBooks don't
    - Smell
    - Feel
- You actually own the book.
    - It is physical. You can touch it
    - You can write in it
    - You can give it away

Conclusion: If you want the complete experience. If you want to immerse yourself in reading. If you want to participate with the author in the beauty of reading then there is no question. Books are better than eReaders.

If you want to use the ancient argument categories for this speech here they are:

Certainty: Studies show the certainty that people understand less when they read on eReaders.

Possibility: It is possible to more easily go back to re-read or move ahead and find your place in a hard copy book.

Credibility: It is credible to believe that if you want the whole emotional experience of a book then the hard copy is best since it involves more senses (touch and smell).

Certainty: Your book is not in the cloud. You own it. You can put your name in it. You can take notes in it, sell it, loan it.

This of course is not as far as you would have to go in constructing arguments. You have to actually make the argument by presenting evidence to show that what you are asserting is true. For example, you would have to show by citing studies that show people comprehend less when using eReaders.

CHAPTER 12

Exercise 7—Commonplace

© Amir Ridhwan/Shutterstock.com

You remember from the discussion of stasis, that a citizen-speaker, for the purpose of focusing the speech topic and finding the bottom-line argument, begins building an argument by asking a question of fact, policy, or value. This exercise teaches the citizen-speaker how to argue for a virtue by arguing against a vice.

Exercise: Argue against a fault or vice. The choice of topic should be a common vice that the culture or society at large believes to be a fault or a vice.

Purpose: The citizen-speaker will learn how to use the pathos proof by arguing against a vice.

The exercise worked like this:

- The speaker would amplify a vice and talk about how much better it was to follow the virtue of which the vice is the opposite.
- This exercise addressed general topics.
- It was an attack on classes of people like tyrants, bullies, drunks, murderers, or gamblers.
- And of course it would praise good rulers, heroes, the sober, and the frugal. And that is why it is called "common."

These vices were "commonly" understood to be wrong or hurtful and their opposite virtues were "commonly" understood to be good or beneficial.

You will not argue the facts of the case here because the facts are a given. They are not in dispute. It is assumed that the virtues/values and the vices are well-known and accepted as such by the audience. This is certainly the assumption the ancient rhetoricians made although it is not necessarily one that can readily be made in twenty-first-century America.

This is where audience analysis comes in handy. A speaker can assess what values are held by the majority of the audience and what the audience considers vices and then make the argument. For example, courage is a virtue generally accepted today and so one would argue against cowardice.

Our old friend Aphthonius gives us the list of how to compose a Commonplace. Here it is:

- Prologue
- Contrary
- Exposition
- Comparison
- Intention
- Digression
- Rejection of pity
- Legality
- Justice
- Advantage
- Possibility

Virtues and vices fall along a continuum. Extreme virtue as well as extreme vice is to be condemned. Here is a short list from Aristotle that explains the continuum.

Aristotle's Ethics

Table of Virtues and Vices

Sphere of Action or Feeling	Excess	Mean	Deficiency
Fear and Confidence	Rashness	Courage	Cowardice
Pleasure and Pain	Licentiousness/Self-indulgence	Temperance	Insensibility
Getting and Spending (minor)	Prodigality	Liberality	Illiberality/Meanness
Getting and Spending (major)	Vulgarity/Tastelessness	Magnificence	Pettiness/Stinginess
Honour and Dishonour (major)	Vanity	Magnanimity	Pusillanimity
Honour and Dishonour (minor)	Ambition/empty vanity	Proper ambition/pride	Unambitiousness/undue humility
Anger	Irascibility	Patience/Good temper	Lack of spirit/unirascibility
Self-expression	Boastfulness	Truthfulness	Understatement/mock modesty
Conversation	Buffoonery	Wittiness	Boorishness
Social Conduct	Obsequiousness	Friendliness	Cantankerousness
Shame	Shyness	Modesty	Shamelessness
Indignation	Envy	Righteous indignation	Malicious enjoyment/Spitefulness
Aristotle (1955). *The Ethics of Aristotle: The Nichomachaen Ethics.* (rev. ed.) (J. K. Thomson, trans.). New York: Viking. p. 104.			

Example of a Commonplace

Gamblers are to be condemned for the harm they do to society.

Prologue: Since gambling can cause misery both to the gambler and his/her family, gambling must be censured.

Contrary: Some consider gambling an enjoyable and harmless pastime that can help people earn money while having fun with friends.

Comparison: Gambling means that the gambler must use money that can easily pay for food and housing for his/her family for her/his own selfish ends. Gambling relies on luck and not on the virtues of hard work and thrift that are the hallmark of the good citizen.

Intention: The gambler is motivated by selfishness and greed. The gambler does not want to work for her/his livelihood. S/He would rather sit all day and eat and drink and play cards, or roll the dice, or pull the lever on a slot machine than do an honest day's labor.

Digression: The gambler has lived a degraded life of always looking for the next big payout. Never thinking of family, never caring about how this constant presence at the gaming tables affects them. The gambler borrows money without hope of repayment or worse steals money when his/her luck runs out to either pay back the gaming house or pay the bills. The gambler is an altogether wretched person.

Rejection of pity: The gambler is not to be pitied. No one forced the gambler to the gaming tables. This person went of her/his own volition. The gambler decided that gambling was to be preferred to the virtues of honesty, thrift, hard work, and responsibility. By this choice the gambler is condemned.

Recall these things:

- **Legality:** If it is wrong to take money from someone when it is not yours then it is wrong to take money from your family for gambling.
- **Justice:** The family needs protection and recompense from the loss of income incurred by the gambler. It is just that s/he should make that recompense.
- **Possibility:** If a friend or family member were to confront the gambler and convince her/him of his/her errors, the gambler could refrain from continuing in this vice.
- **Honor:** The gambler is honor-bound to support and defend the family.

Conclusion: The gambler must be condemned and the virtues of thrift, responsibility, and hard work must be praised.

CHAPTER 13

The Ceremonial Speech
Exercises 8 and 9—Encomium/Invective

The Epideictic or Ceremonial speech is the first of the three broad categories of the Ceremonial speech is generally associated with formal speaking situations. As the name implies, these speeches are given at specific times, during specific events. Examples of such speeches are:

- Wedding toasts
- Convocation addresses
- Commencement addresses
- 911 Remembrances
- Retirement Dinner addresses
- Roasts
- After dinner remarks
- Award acceptances
- Eulogies

While all these events look like they would envoke warm and pleasant words from the speaker, not all ceremonial speeches do. In the progymnasmata, two types of ceremonial speeches were practiced.

- ❏ The Encomium—a speech in praise of a person, place, or thing
- ❏ The Invective—a speech condemning a person, place, or thing

The Encomium

© DeepGreen/Shutterstock.com   © Uncle Leo/Shutterstock.com

This exercise teaches the citizen-speaker how to praise a worthy person, place, or thing. Such speeches, sometime called epideictic speeches, could also praise an idea, a season, a time or epoch, even animals. In modern parlance these speeches are referred to as ceremonial speeches. Such speeches include remarks at special events like 9/11 remembrances, national holiday festivities like the Fourth of July or Labor Day, eulogies, toasts, after dinner remarks, and introductions.

Exercise: Present a glowing picture of the person, place, or thing you wish to praise.

Purpose: To give the citizen-speaker practice in the type of oratory he/she would most likely engage in.

Most of us have probably done one of these at some time or we will be called upon to do them in the future.

- ❏ A wedding toast might be considered an encomium, if one is praising the bride and groom.
- ❏ After dinner speeches are often a praise of someone being honored at a specific occasion.
- ❏ Eulogies praise the person who has died.

This is why the encomium exercise is so important.

Here is how you would go about composing an encomium:

- Prologue—tells the audience who you will speak about
- Describe the person
- Describe the person's deeds
- Compare the person to others to show how praiseworthy the person is
- Epilogue—encourage others to be like this person

Example Encomium

Irene Sendler (1910–2008)

Prologue: Ordinary people do extraordinary things. Such people should be praised for the deeds they do. An ordinary person who did extraordinary things is Irene Sendler.

Describe the person: Irene Sendler was born Irene Krzyanowska on February 15, 1910. Her Roman Catholic parents lived with her in the town of Otwock, Poland, where her father was a doctor. After an uneventful childhood she moved to Warsaw to attend Warsaw University where she studies Polish literature. She was in Warsaw in 1939 when the Nazi Reich attacked Poland, conquered and occupied it. She spent most of the war years in Warsaw where she worked as a Senior Administrator in the Warsaw Social Welfare Department. After the war she remained in Warsaw until her death in May 2008. Irene was married three times, twice to the same man and was the mother of three children.

Describe the deeds of the person: So, Irene Sendler was an ordinary woman. Her deeds, which earned her a Noble Peace Prize nominations in 2006, 2007 and 2008 were not.

- Irene was a member of the Polish Underground who fought against the Nazi occupation of Poland.
- Her job and that of the thirty women who worked with her was to create false documents to aid Polish Jews.
- Eventually she headed the organization assigned to smuggle children out of the Warsaw Ghetto and to safety in convents, orphanages, and gentile families.
- Mrs. Sendler is believed to have on her own smuggled 400 children out of the Warsaw Ghetto.
- Mrs. Sendler and her colleagues are credited with saving over 2,500 children from certain death in Auschwitz and Buchenwald.
- In 1943 she was captured by the Nazis and tortured. She was saved from the firing squad and sent into hiding.
- At the end of the war many of the children she helped save were reunited with their families because Mrs. Sendler and her colleagues kept careful records of who was taken so that the children could be returned to them.

Compare the person with others: Most people would not risk their lives like this. Certainly the Nazis who worked for the extermination of the Jews of Poland and the people who looked the other way are not like Mrs. Sendler and her colleagues.

Epilogue: Elzbieta Ficowska was a baby in 1942. She was one of the many who was rescued from almost certain death by Mrs. Sendler and her colleagues. She lived to grow up and become an ordinary person through the extraordinary deeds of Irene Sendler. She says of this extraordinary woman, "Mrs. Sendler saved not only us, but also our children and grandchildren and the generations to come."

The Invective

This exercise, sometime called Vituperation, is the opposite of the Encomium. In this exercise the citizen-speaker learns to condemn that which s/he believes to be base, unworthy, and/or dangerous. Often these speeches were directed at specific people, but a speaker could also condemn an idea, a vice, or even times and seasons. Most of us have probably done one of these at some time. When we are angry about an issue and speak at the town hall about it or campaign against a candidate, we could be practicing the invective speech.

© Everett Historical/Shutterstock.com

"Classical invective sought to denigrate an individual on the basis of birth, upbringing, 'mechanical' professions, moral defects, physical shortcomings, and so on. It was a branch of epideictic oratory which aimed at undermining the credibility of a judicial witness or political opponent by impugning his integrity. Accordingly, its realm was that of *ethos*, or personal character." (Petrarca)

Exercise: Present a condemnation of a person, place, or thing.

Purpose: To teach the citizen-speaker how to effectively condemn that which the speaker rejects as unworthy.

Here is how you would go about composing an invective:

- Prologue—tells the audience who you will speak about
- Describe the person
- Describe the person's evil deeds
- Compare the person to others to show how evil or disreputable the person is
- Epilogue—encourage others not to emulate this person

Example of an Invective

(This example is based on the characterization of Loki as we see him in the movie *The Avengers*.)

Prologue: Of all the Asgardians, Loki is the worst.

Describe the person: Loki is the adopted son of Odin. His birth father is the Frost Giant Laufey. Loki is a trickster who uses his powers of deception and shape-shifting to evil ends. Loki has a disregard for the lives of those he deems inferior to himself. He is jealous of his brother Thor and believes that he, not Thor, is the rightful king of Asgard.

Describe the person's evil deeds: Loki has many evil deeds to his credit. He uses his shape-shifting abilities to spy on people. He plays tricks on others that cause harm. Loki makes common cause with an evil entity in order to fulfill his dream of becoming a king. His hatred for his brother, Thor, leads him to try to kill him on more than one occasion. He has brought destruction on New York City by opening a space portal that allows an alien army to come to Earth. This army, which Loki leads, killed countless citizens of New York. And finally, Loki has personally killed over eighty people.

Compare to a better person: Loki, of course, would not like the comparison to his brother, but the comparison is apt. Thor has learned to be thoughtful and caring. He uses his great power, not for conquest and subjugation, but for protection and freedom. Thor understands that a king needs to love his people, have compassion on them, fight for them, and if necessary die for them.

Epilogue: Thor is clearly the better person. It is wiser to emulate Thor than his evil brother Loki.

CHAPTER 14

The Informative Speeches
Exercises 10, 11, 12—
Comparison, Descriptive, Characterization

© phloxii/Shutterstock.com

There are three types of informative speeches to choose from in the Progymnasmata. They are

- ❏ Comparison
- ❏ Descriptive
- ❏ Characterization

Each of these speeches is different and requires a different approach. The occasion for the speech has an influence on which of these you will choose when your purpose is to inform.

A speech to the gardening club might be descriptive as you explain where to arrange plants in a shade garden. You would not, most likely put on a persona to give this information. A characterization speech might do better if you are a volunteer at the Harriet Tubman house and museum and you are "playing" a family friend of the period. The comparison lecture on economic systems works in a classroom.

The Comparison Speech

© is am are/Shutterstock.com

The Comparison exercise comes after the encomium and invective because it is actually either a double encomium or an encomium and invective. The point of the **double encomium** is to show which person, place, season, time, animal is greater. You can also highlight the greatness of two great people in a Comparison Speech. The point of the **encomium/invective** is to highlight the greatness of a person by showing how despicable another person is. The speech comparing LeBron to Kobe would fall into the category of double encomium.

Exercise: Double Encomium: Compare two people, places, or things showing which one is the greater. Encomium/Invective: Compare two things praising one and condemning the other.

Purpose: to teach citizen-speakers how to compose speeches which effectively incorporate the first seven exercises in the Progymnasmata. This exercise also teaches citizen-speakers how to convey information in an effective and creative way.

We have already seen how you compose both the encomium and invective speeches:

- Prologue
- Describe the person, idea, place, object, or event
- Describe the deeds of the person or the characteristics of the idea, place, object, or event
- Compare the two
- Epilogue

This is the organization for the Comparison exercise. But there is one additional item to take into account. That is, how to organize the material.

- You can lay out all the information on one person, idea, place, object, or event and then lay out all the information on the second. OR
- You can go point by point, speaking first about one and then about the other. Make sure when you are composing your Comparison that you use parallel points for each.

Example Comparison (Double Encomium)

Introduction: Who in the audience is a *Star Trek* fan? *Star Wars* fan? Like them both? Like neither of them? I ask because there seems to be a rivalry, friendly I hope, between *Star Trek* fans and *Star Wars* fans. Lively discussions ensue about which is better, which is more influential, which will be longest-lasting. Considering that people can lose friendships over this issue maybe we should take a deep breath, calm down, and compare *Star Trek: The Original Series* and *Star Wars: A New Hope*, not to decide which is better, but to show that these culture phenomena are equally matched.

Star Trek began life as a TV series. It premiered on NBC September 8, 1966, ending its run in 1969. The original series led to seven spin-off series: *The Animated Series, The Next Generation, Deep Space Nine, Voyager, Enterprise, Discovery,* and *Short Treks*. The original series and its spin offs have been on TV for over thirty years and have produced more than 725 *Star Trek* episodes. You have probably seen at least one of the thirteen feature films based on the Star Trek universe.

Star Trek: The Original Series is considered Science Fiction. The show centers around space travel, technology and encounters with alien lifeforms. The show is episodic, meaning there is no mythic arc to the story. Each episode stands alone.

Star Wars: A New Hope began life as a movie in 1977. Since then nine films have continued the saga of Luke Skywalker, Leia Organa, and Han Solo. Three spin-off movies, *The Clone Wars, Rogue One,* and *Solo: A Star Wars Story,* take place in the *Star Wars* universe but is not technically part of the succession of the first seven. Three TV specials have been aired using the elements of the *Star Wars* universe.

Star Wars: A New Hope is considered a Science Fantasy. The movie centers around mythological/fantasy themes like the Force, knights, princesses, the battle of good against evil. That all this takes place in space with technologically advanced equipment which is secondary to the main themes of the movie.

Compare the two:
- Both have well-developed universes. The stories take place in worlds that make sense and are consistent.
  - *Star Trek's* world is either the ship (when they didn't have enough money to pay for the sets for an off-ship adventure) or other worlds. These settings have rules that are easy to understand and reproduce for fan fiction and cosplay.

- *Star Wars* has a deep, well-developed backstory that influences all the action that takes place. The Empire is well-defined. The Jedi are believable and recognizable from other stories we know as are the other archetype characters—the young apprentice, the princess, the rogue outlaw with a heart of gold.
- ❏ Both have strong heroes who are young, handsome, strong, and brave and who are not afraid to break the rules when they have to.
  - *Star Trek* has Captain James Tiberius Kirk, who continually breaks the Prime Directive.
  - *Star Wars* has Han Solo, who shoots Greedo first no matter what anyone else tells you.
- ❏ Both have wise men who help the hero win the day.
  - *Star Trek* has Mr. Spock
  - *Star Wars* has Obi Wan Kenobi
- ❏ Both have catch phrases that have become part of our everyday speech
  - *Star Trek* has "Beam me up, Scotty" and "He's dead, Jim."
  - *Star Wars* has "May the Force be with you" and "It's a trap."

Epilogue: The argument about which franchise is better will go on until the stars turn cold. We can see from the comparison made here that there may be a smaller ground for disagreement than we think. Unless we take the discussion one step further and note that, for all they are alike, *Star Trek* doesn't have Jar Jar Binks.

Example Comparison (Encomium/Invective)

Wealth is Better than Fame

Prologue: Wealth is better than fame. You can have one or the other or both, but if you have to choose, wealth is the superior choice.

Describe the person, idea, place, object, or event: According to *investopedia.com* the definition of wealth is "A measure of the value of all of the assets of worth owned by a person, community, company or country." According to *merriam-webster.com* fame is "the condition of being known or recognized by many people."

© Dim Dimich/Shutterstock.com

Describe the deeds of both: Wealth comes in many forms. In this case we are talking about assets that allow a person freedom from want and freedom to give to others. This type of wealth promotes the good of others. Fame also comes in many forms. For our purposes I will define fame as unearned accolades. This kind of fame is an outgrowth of putting oneself in the spotlight regardless of what that spotlight reveals. Fame is the desire to be seen, period. In this case fame promotes selfishness and pride.

© vadimmus/Shutterstock.com

Compare the two: Wealth is clearly better than fame for the following reasons.

- ❏ **Privacy.** Wealth can afford you privacy to do as you like. Fame constantly keeps you in the public eye where you have to put up with prying photographers, tabloid stories which may be true or untrue, and stalker fans. Fame covets this access: The more, the better.

- ❏ **Longevity**. Carefully invested and cautiously spent, wealth can be with you for your lifetime and then be passed on to your heirs. No truer words were ever spoken than "all glory is fleeting." Who remembers Paris Hilton? Who will remember Honey Boo Boo? Who wants to remember them?
- ❏ **Charity**. Wealth allows you to give to charity and really make a difference. Fame does not mean you have assets that allow for charitable works. Fame spends your money keeping you famous. There is a reason Mike Tyson blew through his reportedly 400 million dollars.

Epilogue: People are often asked which they prefer wealth or fame. Some want both. But they should look more carefully at that choice. By all measures wealth is a better option than fame.

The Descriptive Speech

© Alexander Tihonov/Shutterstock.com

These speeches are simple, straight-forward descriptions of people, place, things, times, events, seasons, and anything else that might lend itself to being talked about from head to toe. It appears to be a sad fact that most people skip the descriptions in novels. And that is a shame since authors spend time working to make their settings come alive. JRR Tolkien, author of the *Lord of the Rings*, comes to mind in this respect. If you favor descriptive speeches you should take the time to read good examples of descriptive writing in your favorite books.

Our favorite teachers of the Progymnasmata have this to say about description:

- ❏ Aphthonius: "[description] is an expository speech, distinctly presenting to view the thing being set forth."
- ❏ Hermogenes: [descriptions bring] "before one's eyes what is being shown."

So what that all means is that your speech is designed to show through words what you have seen. You do this all the time with friends when you:

- ❏ Describe your day
- ❏ Explain how you rearranged your room

- ❏ Walk your friend through an outstanding play by your favorite team
- ❏ Talk about what someone looks like

Exercise: Describe a person, place, or thing using a standard organizational pattern (left to right; head to toe; back to front; first to last).

Purpose: The audience will be able to imagine clearly what the citizen-speaker is describing. This exercise taught the citizen-speaker:

- ❏ How to bring narratives to life
- ❏ How to describe people, places, and things so as to bring more life to the previous two exercises

This exercise is not as easy as it might first appear. The citizen-speaker is required to think about what aspects of the thing described **needs** to be included and then how to talk about those in a way the audience can understand.

Example Description

Zombies

Introduction: Since the Zombie Apocalypse may come any day it is important to know who you are dealing with. You can spot a zombie a mile away (mostly because they walk verrrry slooowly). Here is a short guide to zombiehood.

Narrative: Let's begin with some basics:

- ❏ A zombie is an undead whose body is in a state of decomposition. That means that the zombie is falling apart.
- ❏ The zombie can't speak, think, or reason. This makes communicating with other zombies really hard.
- ❏ The zombie has no conscience or free will and lacks a soul. Therefore the zombie is not human.
- ❏ The typical zombie weapons are hands and teeth.

© Timofeev Sergey/Shutterstock.com

Now we can look at zombie physiology and biology:

- ❏ They kill people
- ❏ They have blank expressions
- ❏ They wear clothes but only those clothes they were wearing when they became zombies
- ❏ They seem to be stronger than living human beings
- ❏ They do not feel pain
- ❏ They do not need to eat or drink
- ❏ They can be killed. (And you probably know how to do it without my telling you.)

Conclusion: Now you know what zombies look like. This information will be helpful to you in the event of the zombie apocalypse.

The Characterization Speech

© Chris Harvey/Shutterstock.com

This exercise is probably the most difficult one in the Progymnasmata. A characterization/Impersonation speech requires the citizen-speaker to "take on" the personality or character of a real or fictional person and argue a proposition or relate information from that person's point of view.

Cosplay and historic re-enacting as well as groups like the Society for Creative Anachronism contain real-life examples of the exercise. The picture above shows a group of cosplayers impersonating characters from the British TV series **Dr Who**.

Exercise: The citizen-speaker will use the ethos of the impersonated character to support a proposition or impart information.

Purpose: To encourage the audience to think, believe, or do something because they identify with and wish to emulate (or conversely do not identify with and wish to avoid the behaviors) of the impersonated character.

This is essentially a creative writing exercise that allows you to use invented dialogue. Examples of this exercise are easily found in pop culture.

- ❏ Historical—any biopic
    - *Stand and Deliver* (Jaime Escalante)
    - *What's Love Got to Do With It* (Ike and Tina Turner)
    - *42* (Jackie Robinson)
    - *Saving Mr. Banks* (PL Travers and Walt Disney)
    - *300* (Xerxes and Leonidas)

- ❏ Legendary
    - Perseus from the *Clash of the Titan* movies
    - Hercules from any movie you care to name
    - Cleopatra from any movie or Shakespeare play

- Imaginary
    - Katniss Everdeen from *The Hunger Games*
    - Hermione Granger from the *Harry Potter* series
    - Frodo Baggins from the *Lord of the Rings*

Other ways of approaching this exercise are to:

- Invent your own character
- Invent dialog/monologue for a friend or family member

Or you can compose a monologue or dialogue based on stock characters

- The Yuppie
- The Gutsy Heroine
- The Geek/Nerd
- The Smart Aleck Kid
- The Clueless Dad
- The Wise Doctor
- The Urban Hipster
- The "red shirt" (This is a reference to the extras that get killed in the first ten minutes of a TV show or movie. The red shirt as a throw-away character was introduced in the original 1960s *Star Trek* series.)
- The Stoner
- The "Salt of the Earth"

This exercise requires:

- Either a monologue (one person speaking) or a dialogue (two people speaking).
- That you either compose the monologue or dialogue yourself, or find a monologue or dialogue that makes your point and use that. (You must cite the source of the impersonation if you did not write it yourself.)
- That the monologues or dialogues be fictitious. They cannot have actually taken place.
- That you make a point by putting words into the mouths of others, as long as those words are consistent with the who that person actually thought, what that person actually believed, and how that person actually acted.
- That you act out this dialogue in the speech, giving you more dramatic leeway than any other exercise in the Progymnasmata.

Remember that you are creating characters here. You want to show who a person is by what that person says and how that person speaks. By doing this well, you can convey a message without hammering someone with it. This is a clever devise for getting your point across.

Students choosing to do this exercise have in the past impersonated:

- Han Solo, who retold the Star Wars saga from his point-of-view
- Malcolm X, who "read" a letter to his daughter
- Nelson Mandela, who spoke against what is currently happening in South Africa
- A Civil War soldier, who was the student-speaker's ancestor. We learned what it was like to be a Union soldier during this conflict
- A student who explained deductive reasoning through a dramatic recitation of the "mobile phone" monologue from the British TV series *Sherlock*.

Example Impersonation/Characterization

© Zwiebackesser/Shutterstock.com

Do you have any idea what it is like to be the "Goddess of Love"? Well I do and I can tell you it is no picnic. Oh, Aphrodite you're so beautiful. Oh Aphrodite can you make so and so love me. Oh, Aphrodite can you tell me your secret?

Thanks.

No.

And absolutely, no.

Next question? The whole thing is a nuisance.

You think it is a walk in the park to be like me? How would you like to have been born of sea foam? Well, I have to say that that great painting of me standing on that sea shell coming up out of the water is pretty nice. Here it is.

[insert slide of the Botticelli painting]

What do you think? I am really beautiful, you know.

And then I get all these silly attributes like a dove and a mirror and an apple and a scallop shell. Here they all are.

[insert slide of attributes]

The mirror I get because I am so very attractive, but the others? Really?

My biggest problem is that I am always getting into trouble because I am so very lovely. Absolutely lovely.

Look who I am married to.

[insert slide of Hyphaestus]

Is it any wonder that I had a little fling with Ares?

And it is true that I really, really liked Adonis and Ankhises. But I don't think that should be held against me.

[insert slides of Adonis and Ankhises]

And the Trojan War was not my fault. Just because Paris thought I was the prettiest (and how could he not) and gave me the golden apple (which you remember is one of my attributes so how could he not).

Now it's possible that he gave me the apple because I did make a little promise to him that he could have Helen as his wife. So she was married to some king. And so what if Paris had to kidnap her. Nobody had to go to war over that. If they did that was their choice.

[Insert slide of Helen and Paris]

Don't they look great together?

Of course in the end Homer wrote this great poem about it. So it all worked out.

Oh, is that the time! I have to go see Pygmalion. He wants me to bring this statue to life for him. A goddess's, work is never done.

* * *

So what did you discover from this short impersonation?

- ❏ Who Aphrodite is
- ❏ Who she is married to
- ❏ A little bit of her history
- ❏ A little bit of her personality

It would be easy enough to do a Descriptive speech on this Greek goddess. But it is more interesting and fun to do the description by placing the words in her mouth and letting her speak for herself.

Oh and one other thing. Notice that there are places in this speech where visuals are used. They are spread throughout the speech and are used to enhance the message.

Example Dialogue

The Adventure of the Bruce-Partington Plans (A Sherlock Holmes Story)
by Sir Arthur Conan Doyle

> "The London criminal is certainly a dull fellow," said he in the querulous voice . . . "Look out this window, Watson. . . The thief or the murderer could roam London on such a day as the tiger does the jungle, unseen until he pounces. . ."

> "There have," said I, "been numerous petty thefts."

> Holmes snorted his contempt.

> "This great and sombre stage is set for something more worthy than that," said he. "It is fortunate for this community that I am not a criminal."

> "It is, indeed!" said I heartily.

Source: Public Domain

"Suppose that I were Brooks or Woodhouse, or any of the fifty men who have good reason for taking my life, how long could I survive against my own pursuit? A summons, a bogus appointment, and all would be over . . . By Jove! here comes something at last to break our dead monotony."

It was the maid with a telegram. Holmes tore it open and burst out laughing.

"Well, well! What next?" said he. "Brother Mycroft is coming round."

"Why not?" I asked.

"Why not? It is as if you met a tram-car coming down a country lane. Mycroft has his rails and he runs on them. . . Once, and only once, he has been here. What upheaval can possibly have derailed him?"

"Does he not explain?"

Holmes handed me his brother's telegram.

Must see you over Cadogen West. Coming at once.

Mycroft.

"Cadogen West? I have heard the name."

"It recalls nothing to my mind. But that Mycroft should break out in this erratic fashion! A planet might as well leave its orbit. By the way, do you know what Mycroft is?"

. . . "You told me that he had some small office under the British government."

Holmes chuckled.

". . .You are right in thinking that he is under the British government. You would also be right in a sense if you said that occasionally he IS the British government."

"My dear Holmes!"

"I thought I might surprise you. Mycroft draws four hundred and fifty pounds a year, remains a subordinate, has no ambitions of any kind, will receive neither honour nor title, but remains the most indispensable man in the country . . . Again and again his word has decided the national policy. He lives in it. He thinks of nothing else save when, as an intellectual exercise, he unbends if I call upon him and ask him to advise me on one of my little problems. But Jupiter is descending to-day. What on earth can it mean? Who is Cadogan West, and what is he to Mycroft?"

"I have it," I cried, and plunged among the litter of papers upon the sofa. "Yes, yes, here he is, sure enough! Cadogan West was the young man who was found dead on the Underground on Tuesday morning."

Holmes sat up at attention, his pipe halfway to his lips.

"This must be serious, Watson. A death which has caused my brother to alter his habits can be no ordinary one. What in the world can he have to do with it?" . . .

"There has been an inquest," said I, "and a good many fresh facts have come out. Looked at more closely, I should certainly say that it was a curious case."

"Judging by its effect upon my brother, I should think it must be a most extraordinary one." He snuggled down in his armchair. "Now, Watson, let us have the facts."

"The man's name was Arthur Cadogan West. He was twenty-seven years of age, unmarried, and a clerk at Woolwich Arsenal."

"He left Woolwich suddenly on Monday night. . .The next thing heard of him was when his dead body was discovered by a plate-layer named Mason, just outside Aldgate Station on the Underground system in London."

"When?"

"The body was found at six on Tuesday morning. . ."

"Very good. The case is definite enough. The man, dead or alive, either fell or was precipitated from a train. So much is clear to me. Continue."

. . . "There was no ticket in his pockets."

"No ticket! Dear me, Watson, this is really very singular. According to my experience it is not possible to reach the platform of a Metropolitan train without exhibiting one's ticket."

". . . There is a list here of his possessions. His purse contained two pounds fifteen. He had also a check-book on the Woolwich branch of the Capital and Counties Bank. Through this his identity was established. There were also two dress-circle tickets for the Woolwich Theatre, dated for that very evening. Also a small packet of technical papers."

Holmes gave an exclamation of satisfaction.

"There we have it at last, Watson! British government—Woolwich. Arsenal—technical papers—Brother Mycroft, the chain is complete. But here he comes, if I am not mistaken, to speak for himself." (Conan Doyle)

This dialogue, while long, can be made shorter. Indeed as you can see by the repeated ellipses in the dialogue this dialogue was cut to fit a time limit. As long as you don't change the meaning, you can make the text as short as you need to.

What do you learn about Holmes and Watson from this dialogue?

- ❏ Holmes is bored
- ❏ Watson is intelligent
- ❏ Holmes has a difficult relationship with his brother

How would you use this as a speech and what would you be trying to prove?

- ❏ Sherlock Holmes can be used as an ethos argument. Even though he is a fictional character people respect his brains.
- ❏ Holmes can be used as the chief exponent of logos arguments. Notice the reasoning Holmes uses to reach his conclusions.
- ❏ The whole dialogue can be seen as an exercise in deductive reasoning.

CHAPTER 15

The Persuasive Speech
The Deliberative and Forensic Exercises
Exercises 13 and 14
Thesis and the Introduction to Law

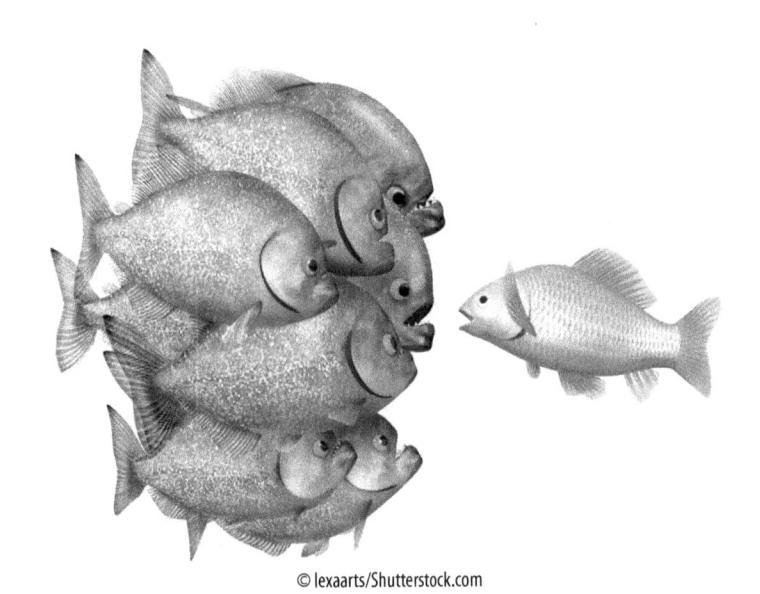

The Progymnasmata ends with two persuasive speech exercises. These roughly conform to the Deliberative (Policy) and Forensic (legal) speech types first outlined by Aristotle. The Progymnasmata calls these speeches

- ❏ Thesis
- ❏ Introduction to Law

The persuasive speech purpose is to move the audience from point A, what they already think, believe, or do, to point B, what you want the audience to think, believe, or do. The citizen-speaker's job is to

- ❏ Develop a narrow purpose
- ❏ Research and select the best evidence to support that purpose
- ❏ Construct cogent arguments in support of that purpose
- ❏ Give the audience a reason to want to be persuaded by the arguments you selected

The Thesis Speech

The Thesis exercise was designed to answer a general question. Specific questions were regarded as hypotheticals and would fall outside the parameters of this exercise.

Exercise: Ask a question and argue for the answer you choose. This exercise requires the citizen-speaker to present arguments on both sides of the issue.

Purpose: To teach the citizen-speaker how to argue a position using as many of the first seven exercises as necessary to support the position being argued. This exercise incorporates the understanding of ethos, pathos, and logos that the citizen-speaker studied up to this point.

In modern terms the thesis exercise is a persuasive speech. Such questions as:

- Should students go on vacation during spring break?
- Should one take out loans to go to college?
- Should people be required to get a license to have children?

You can set up this exercise in the same way you would a typical persuasive speech. Here is the classical pattern of arrangement or organization as we call it today:

- Introduction
- Narration
- Confirmation
- Disputation
- Conclusion

If you want to make it easier you can do the following:

- Problem/Solution
- Advantages/Disadvantages

For the Problem/Solution Arrangement you would

- Introduce the speech
- Lay out the problem
- Offer a solution
- Conclude

If you choose to do a problem/solution speech you should look back on our discussion of argument and think carefully about solvency. The solution you propose for the problem you outline must work and it must not cause more problems than it fixes.

For the Advantages/Disadvantages you would

- ❑ Introduce the speech
- ❑ Lay out the advantages
- ❑ Lay out the disadvantages
- ❑ Conclusion

Practice Thesis

Should elementary schoolchildren be required to learn cursive writing?

© karen roach/Shutterstock.com

Introduction: Should elementary schoolchildren be required to learn cursive writing? When I was young no one would have given such a question a second thought. Or even a first thought. But this question is being asked now and the answer is a resounding "no". But should that be the answer? Should we still be teaching cursive to young children? Of course we should.

Narrative: There was a time when putting pen to paper was the only form of written communication available. And even after the advent of the typewriter handwritten communication was still important. But today we don't need to write much by hand. So much is done on computers that learning good penmanship and writing legibly seem no longer necessary. So why should children learn this old-fashioned method?

Confirmation: Here is why:

- ❑ Cursive writing is a skill. Skills-based knowledge is more important than knowledge for knowledge's sake.
- ❑ Cursive writing is beautiful, encourages creativity, and helps student develop a unique signature.
- ❑ Cursive writing allows one to read old documents and connect with the past.

Refutation: Opponents of cursive writing education will say:

- Cursive writing is obsolete. With the advent of the computer learning to write by hand is no longer an important skill.
- Cursive writing is an art form. Art should be saved for art classes.
- Cursive writing takes up too much class time that could be better spent on more important material.

Conclusion: While it is true that learning to write well is time-consuming and that one can get along without an artistic signature these are not reasons to abandon the teaching of cursive writing. The benefits of learning this skill far outweigh the costs. We should return to the time-honored practice of teaching cursive writing to elementary school children.

The Introduction to Law Speech

In this final exercise the citizen-speaker was to praise or denounce a law. As with all of the exercises the citizen-speaker was to present both sides of the issue and then make clear which side is to be preferred.

Exercise: Using a real or fictitious law present the pros and cons for the law and argue for one side or the other.

Purpose: To teach the citizen-speaker how to present a good argument for or against the laws under which the citizen-speaker lives.

There are questions you can ask yourself about laws when engaged in this exercise. The original list of questions come to us from Quintilian.

- Was the law clearly written?
- Is it consistent within itself?
- Is the law just?
- Is it expedient? An expedient law may advocate doing something in the most convenient and advantageous manner, but also violates standard ethical considerations. You would argue either
    - That the law should be repealed because of these ethical considerations
    - That the law should stand despite these ethical considerations
- Can it be enforced? Categories of unenforceable laws
    - Behavior: Can the government prevent people from giving their children a glass of wine in their own homes?
    - Obscure: In Oklahoma, you can be arrested for making ugly faces at a dog.
    - Impossible: In New York, the penalty for jumping off a building is death.

The question about enforcement is a particularly interesting one. For instance a subset question under enforcement might be: is the law selectively enforced?

Other questions you might cover in your exercise are:

- ❏ Is the law practical?
- ❏ Is the law decent?

The easiest way to do this exercise is to:

- ❏ Introduce the law
- ❏ Pick a couple of the questions above to answer
- ❏ Answer them
- ❏ Conclusion

The Amendments to the Constitution of the United States

The Amendments to the US Constitution works well for this exercise as some of them are still in dispute

- ❏ The 16th Amendment
- ❏ The 17th Amendment

Both of these have constituencies that would like to see them abolished.

Another way of approaching this exercise is to propose a new amendment to the Constitution.

- ❏ Balanced Budget
- ❏ Term Limits

Here are the 27 Amendments

Here we go.

The 1st Ten are Called the Bill of Rights

Amendment I

Congress shall make no law respecting an establishment of religion, or prohibiting the free exercise thereof; or abridging the freedom of speech, or of the press; or the right of the people peaceably to assemble, and to petition the Government for a redress of grievances.

Amendment II

A well regulated Militia, being necessary to the security of a free State, the right of the people to keep and bear Arms, shall not be infringed.

Amendment III

No Soldier shall, in time of peace be quartered in any house, without the consent of the Owner, nor in time of war, but in a manner to be prescribed by law.

Amendment IV

The right of the people to be secure in their persons, houses, papers, and effects, against unreasonable searches and seizures, shall not be violated, and no Warrants shall issue, but upon probable cause, supported by Oath or affirmation, and particularly describing the place to be searched, and the persons or things to be seized.

Amendment V

No person shall be held to answer for a capital, or otherwise infamous crime, unless on a presentment or indictment of a Grand Jury, except in cases arising in the land or naval forces, or in the Militia, when in actual service in time of War or public danger; nor shall any person be subject for the same offence to be twice put in jeopardy of life or limb; nor shall be compelled in any criminal case to be a witness against himself, nor be deprived of life, liberty, or property, without due process of law; nor shall private property be taken for public use, without just compensation.

Amendment VI

In all criminal prosecutions, the accused shall enjoy the right to a speedy and public trial, by an impartial jury of the State and district wherein the crime shall have been committed, which district shall have been previously ascertained by law, and to be informed of the nature and cause of the accusation; to be confronted with the witnesses against him; to have compulsory process for obtaining witnesses in his favor, and to have the Assistance of Counsel for his defense.

Amendment VII

In suits at common law, where the value in controversy shall exceed twenty dollars, the right of trial by jury shall be preserved, and no fact tried by a jury, shall be otherwise reexamined in any Court of the United States, than according to the rules of the common law.

Amendment VIII

Excessive bail shall not be required, nor excessive fines imposed, nor cruel and unusual punishments inflicted.

Amendment IX

The enumeration in the Constitution, of certain rights, shall not be construed to deny or disparage others retained by the people.

Amendment X

The powers not delegated to the United States by the Constitution, nor prohibited by it to the States, are reserved to the States respectively, or to the people.

The next 17 are the Changes and Additions to the Constitution.

Amendment XI

Note: Article III, section 2, of the Constitution was modified by amendment 11.

The Judicial power of the United States shall not be construed to extend to any suit in law or equity, commenced or prosecuted against one of the United States by Citizens of another State, or by Citizens or Subjects of any Foreign State.

Amendment XII

Note: A portion of Article II, section 1 of the Constitution was superseded by the 12th amendment.

The Electors shall meet in their respective states and vote by ballot for President and Vice-President, one of whom, at least, shall not be an inhabitant of the same state with themselves; they shall name in their ballots the person voted for as President, and in distinct ballots the person voted for as Vice-President, and they shall make distinct lists of all persons voted for as President, and of all persons voted for as Vice-President, and of the number of votes for each, which lists they shall sign and certify, and transmit sealed to the seat of the government of the United States, directed to the President of the Senate;—the President of the Senate shall, in the presence of the Senate and House of Representatives, open all the certificates and the votes shall then be counted;—The person having the greatest number of votes for President, shall be the President, if such number be a majority of the whole number of Electors appointed; and if no person have such majority, then from the persons having the highest numbers not exceeding three on the list of those voted for as President, the House of Representatives shall choose immediately, by ballot, the President. But in choosing the President, the votes shall be taken by states, the representation from each state having one vote; a quorum for this purpose shall consist of a member or members from two-thirds of the states, and a majority of all the states shall be necessary to a choice. [And if the House of Representatives shall not choose a President whenever the right of choice shall devolve upon them, before the fourth day of March next following, then the Vice-President shall act as President, as in case of the death or other constitutional disability of the President.—]* The person having the greatest number of votes as Vice-President, shall be the Vice-President, if such number be a majority of the whole number of Electors appointed, and if no person have a majority, then from the two highest numbers on the list, the Senate shall choose the Vice-President; a quorum for the purpose shall consist of two-thirds of the whole number of Senators, and a majority of the whole number shall be necessary to a choice. But no person constitutionally ineligible to the office of President shall be eligible to that of Vice-President of the United States.

*Section 3 of the 20th amendment changes this amendment.

Amendment XIII

Note: A portion of Article IV, section 2, of the Constitution was superseded by the 13th amendment.

Section 1. Neither slavery nor involuntary servitude, except as a punishment for crime whereof the party shall have been duly convicted, shall exist within the United States, or any place subject to their jurisdiction.

Section 2. Congress shall have power to enforce this article by appropriate legislation.

Amendment XIV

Section 1. All persons born or naturalized in the United States, and subject to the jurisdiction thereof, are citizens of the United States and of the State wherein they reside. No State shall make or enforce any law which shall abridge the privileges or immunities of citizens of the United States; nor shall any State deprive any person of life, liberty, or property, without due process of law; nor deny to any person within its jurisdiction the equal protection of the laws.

Section 2. Representatives shall be apportioned among the several States according to their respective numbers, counting the whole number of persons in each State, excluding Indians not taxed. But when the right to vote at any election for the choice of electors for President and Vice-President of the United States, Representatives in Congress, the Executive and Judicial officers of a State, or the members of the Legislature thereof, is denied to any of the male inhabitants of such State, being twenty-one years of age,* and citizens of the United States, or in any way abridged, except for participation in rebellion, or other crime, the basis of representation therein shall be reduced in the proportion which the number of such male citizens shall bear to the whole number of male citizens twenty-one years of age in such State.

Section 3. No person shall be a Senator or Representative in Congress, or elector of President and Vice-President, or hold any office, civil or military, under the United States, or under any State, who, having previously taken an oath, as a member of Congress, or as an officer of the United States, or as a member of any State legislature, or as an executive or judicial officer of any State, to support the Constitution of the United States, shall have engaged in insurrection or rebellion against the same, or given aid or comfort to the enemies thereof. But Congress may by a vote of two-thirds of each House, remove such disability.

Section 4. The validity of the public debt of the United States, authorized by law, including debts incurred for payment of pensions and bounties for services in suppressing insurrection or rebellion, shall not be questioned. But neither the United States nor any State shall assume or pay any debt or obligation incurred in aid of insurrection or rebellion against the United States, or any claim for the loss or emancipation of any slave; but all such debts, obligations and claims shall be held illegal and void.

Section 5. The Congress shall have the power to enforce, by appropriate legislation, the provisions of this article.

Changed by section 1 of the 26th amendment.

Amendment XV

Section 1. The right of citizens of the United States to vote shall not be denied or abridged by the United States or by any State on account of race, color, or previous condition of servitude—

Section 2. The Congress shall have the power to enforce this article by appropriate legislation.

Amendment XVI

Note: Article I, section 9, of the Constitution was changed by this amendment.

The Congress shall have power to lay and collect taxes on incomes, from whatever source derived, without apportionment among the several States, and without regard to any census or enumeration.

Amendment XVII

Note: This changed Article I, section 3, of the Constitution, which outlined how senators were to be appointed.

The Senate of the United States shall be composed of two Senators from each State, elected by the people thereof, for six years; and each Senator shall have one vote. The electors in each State shall have the qualifications requisite for electors of the most numerous branch of the State legislatures.

When vacancies happen in the representation of any State in the Senate, the executive authority of such State shall issue writs of election to fill such vacancies: Provided, That the legislature of any State may empower the executive thereof to make temporary appointments until the people fill the vacancies by election as the legislature may direct.

This amendment shall not be so construed as to affect the election or term of any Senator chosen before it becomes valid as part of the Constitution.

Amendment XVIII

Section 1. After one year from the ratification of this article the manufacture, sale, or transportation of intoxicating liquors within, the importation thereof into, or the exportation thereof from the United States and all territory subject to the jurisdiction thereof for beverage purposes is hereby prohibited.

Section 2. The Congress and the several States shall have concurrent power to enforce this article by appropriate legislation.

Section 3. This article shall be inoperative unless it shall have been ratified as an amendment to the Constitution by the legislatures of the several States, as provided in the Constitution, within seven years from the date of the submission hereof to the States by the Congress.

Amendment XIX

The right of citizens of the United States to vote shall not be denied or abridged by the United States or by any State on account of sex.

Congress shall have power to enforce this article by appropriate legislation.

Amendment XX

Section 1. The terms of the President and the Vice President shall end at noon on the 20th day of January, and the terms of Senators and Representatives at noon on the 3d day of January, of the years in which such terms would have ended if this article had not been ratified; and the terms of their successors shall then begin.

Section 2. The Congress shall assemble at least once in every year, and such meeting shall begin at noon on the 3d day of January, unless they shall by law appoint a different day.

Section 3. If, at the time fixed for the beginning of the term of the President, the President elect shall have died, the Vice President elect shall become President. If a President shall not have been chosen before the time fixed for the beginning of his term, or if the President elect shall have failed to qualify, then the Vice President elect shall act as President until a President shall have qualified; and the Congress may by law provide for the case wherein neither a President elect nor a Vice President shall have qualified, declaring who shall then act as President, or the manner in which one who is to act shall be selected, and such person shall act accordingly until a President or Vice President shall have qualified.

Section 4. The Congress may by law provide for the case of the death of any of the persons from whom the House of Representatives may choose a President whenever the right of choice shall have devolved upon them, and for the case of the death of any of the persons from whom the Senate may choose a Vice President whenever the right of choice shall have devolved upon them.

Section 5. Sections 1 and 2 shall take effect on the 15th day of October following the ratification of this article.

Section 6. This article shall be inoperative unless it shall have been ratified as an amendment to the Constitution by the legislatures of three-fourths of the several States within seven years from the date of its submission.

Amendment XXI

Section 1. The eighteenth article of amendment to the Constitution of the United States is hereby repealed.

Section 2. The transportation or importation into any State, Territory, or Possession of the United States for delivery or use therein of intoxicating liquors, in violation of the laws thereof, is hereby prohibited.

Section 3. This article shall be inoperative unless it shall have been ratified as an amendment to the Constitution by conventions in the several States, as provided in the Constitution, within seven years from the date of the submission hereof to the States by the Congress.

Amendment XXII

Section 1. No person shall be elected to the office of the President more than twice, and no person who has held the office of President, or acted as President, for more than two years of a term to which some other person was elected President shall be elected to the office of President more than once. But this Article shall not apply to any person holding the office of President when this Article was proposed by Congress, and shall not prevent any person who may be holding the office of President, or acting as President, during the term within which this Article becomes operative from holding the office of President or acting as President during the remainder of such term.

Section 2. This article shall be inoperative unless it shall have been ratified as an amendment to the Constitution by the legislatures of three-fourths of the several States within seven years from the date of its submission to the States by the Congress.

Amendment XXIII

Section 1. The District constituting the seat of Government of the United States shall appoint in such manner as Congress may direct:

A number of electors of President and Vice President equal to the whole number of Senators and Representatives in Congress to which the District would be entitled if it were a State, but in no event more than the least populous State; they shall be in addition to those appointed by the States, but they shall be considered, for the purposes of the election of President and Vice President, to be electors appointed by a State; and they shall meet in the District and perform such duties as provided by the twelfth article of amendment.

Section 2. The Congress shall have power to enforce this article by appropriate legislation.

Amendment XXIV

Section 1. The right of citizens of the United States to vote in any primary or other election for President or Vice President, for electors for President or Vice President, or for Senator or Representative in Congress, shall not be denied or abridged by the United States or any State by reason of failure to pay poll tax or other tax.

Section 2. The Congress shall have power to enforce this article by appropriate legislation.

Amendment XXV

Section 1. In case of the removal of the President from office or of his death or resignation, the Vice President shall become President.

Section 2. Whenever there is a vacancy in the office of the Vice President, the President shall nominate a Vice President who shall take office upon confirmation by a majority vote of both Houses of Congress.

Section 3. Whenever the President transmits to the President pro tempore of the Senate and the Speaker of the House of Representatives his written declaration that he is unable to discharge the powers and duties of his office, and until he transmits to them a written declaration to the contrary, such powers and duties shall be discharged by the Vice President as Acting President.

Section 4. Whenever the Vice President and a majority of either the principal officers of the executive departments or of such other body as Congress may by law provide, transmit to the President pro tempore of the Senate and the Speaker of the House of Representatives their written declaration that the President is unable to discharge the powers and duties of his office, the Vice President shall immediately assume the powers and duties of the office as Acting President.

Thereafter, when the President transmits to the President pro tempore of the Senate and the Speaker of the House of Representatives his written declaration that no inability exists, he shall resume the powers and duties of his office unless the Vice President and a majority of either the principal officers of the executive department or of such other body as Congress may by law provide, transmit within four days to the President pro tempore of the Senate and the Speaker of the House of Representatives their written declaration that the President is unable to discharge the powers and duties of his office. Thereupon Congress shall decide the issue, assembling within forty-eight hours for that purpose if not in session. If the Congress, within twenty-one days after receipt of the latter written declaration, or, if Congress is not in session, within twenty-one days after Congress is required to assemble, determines by two-thirds vote of both Houses that the President is unable to discharge the powers and duties of his office, the Vice President shall continue to discharge the same as Acting President; otherwise, the President shall resume the powers and duties of his office.

Amendment XXVI

Section 1. The right of citizens of the United States, who are eighteen years of age or older, to vote shall not be denied or abridged by the United States or by any State on account of age.

Section 2: Congress shall have the power to enforce this article by appropriate legislation.

Amendment XXVII

No law, varying the compensation for the services of the Senators and Representatives, shall take effect, until an election of representatives shall have intervened.

Example Introduction to Law

"The Great Commoner"

William Jennings Bryan

We will use what is considered the most famous speech in American political history for our example here. The speech was delivered by William Jennings Bryan at the Democratic National Convention, July, 9, 1896. The speech has become known as "The Cross of Gold Speech." It was such a powerful oration that Bryan was nominated by that convention to run for president that year. He lost, but was nominated again in 1900 and 1908, alas for him losing both times. He never did become president.

The issue:

- ❏ Would the United States continue to back its paper money with gold or
- ❏ Would the United States use silver and gold as backing for the paper dollar.
- ❏ Bryan was a silver and gold proponent.

Courtesy Library of Congress, catalog number LC-USZ62-8425.

The "law" Bryan was arguing against was a plank in the Democratic Platform that would have endorsed the "gold only" approach.

If you know anything about this speech you know this: **"You shall not press down upon the brow of labor this crown of thorns, you shall not crucify mankind upon a cross of gold."**

This is a long speech and the language can be difficult because of the way people strung their words together in those days. But hang in there. Bryan was an accomplished speaker and it is well worth your time to read the entire speech.

You can see parts of the Progymnasmata in this speech, by the way. And fortunately for us, the speech is set up in the classical organizational pattern. We have made editorial notes in the text of the speech. These appear in brackets.

Exordium/Introduction:
- ❏ I would be presumptuous, indeed, to present myself against the distinguished gentlemen to whom you have listened if this were a mere measuring of abilities; [beginning to build ethos] but this is not a contest between persons. The humblest citizen in all the land, when clad in the armor of a righteous cause, is stronger than all the hosts of error [values argument and audience identification]. I come to speak to you in defense of a cause as holy as the cause of liberty—the cause of humanity [values argument].
- ❏ When this debate is concluded, a motion will be made to lay upon the table the resolution offered in commendation of the Administration, and also, the resolution offered in condemnation of the Administration.
  - ▪ We object to bringing this question down to the level of persons.
  - ▪ The individual is but an atom; he is born, he acts, he dies; but principles are eternal; and this has been a contest over a principle [beginning of a commonplace argument].

Narratio/Narrative: Never before in the history of this country has there been witnessed such a contest as that through which we have just passed.

- ❏ Never before in the history of American politics has a great issue been fought out as this issue has been, by the voters of a great party [audience identification].
- ❏ On the fourth of March 1895, a few Democrats, most of them members of Congress, issued an address to the Democrats of the nation,
  - ▪ **asserting** that the money question was the paramount issue of the hour;
  - ▪ **declaring** that a majority of the Democratic party had the right to control the action of the party on this paramount issue; and
  - ▪ **concluding** with the request that the believers in the free coinage of silver in the Democratic party should organize, take charge of, and control the policy of the Democratic party. [type of anaphora]
- ❏ Three months later, at Memphis, an organization was perfected, and the silver Democrats went forth openly and courageously proclaiming their belief, and declaring that, if successful, they would crystallize into a platform the declaration which they had made.
- ❏ Then began the struggle. With a zeal approaching the zeal which inspired the Crusaders who followed Peter the Hermit, our silver Democrats went forth from victory unto victory until they are now assembled, not to discuss, not to debate, but to enter up the judgment already rendered by the plain people of this country [chreia].
- ❏ In this contest brother has been arrayed against brother, father against son.
  - ▪ The warmest ties of love, acquaintance, and association have been disregarded;
  - ▪ old leaders have been cast aside when they have refused to give expression to the sentiments of those whom they would lead, and
  - ▪ new leaders have sprung up to give direction to this cause of truth. Thus has the contest been waged, and we have assembled here under as binding and solemn instructions as were ever imposed upon representatives of the people.
- ❏ We do not come as individuals. As individuals we might have been glad to compliment the gentleman from New York [Senator Hill], but we know that the people for whom we speak would never be willing to put him in a position where he could thwart the will of the Democratic party.
- ❏ I say it was not a question of persons; it was a question of principle, and it is not with gladness, my friends, that we find ourselves brought into conflict with those who are now arrayed on the other side. [invective]

Refutation: When you [turning to the gold delegates] come before us and tell us that we are about to disturb your business interests, we reply that you have disturbed our business interests by your course.

- [The law is not just] We say to you that you have made the definition of a business man too limited in its application.
    - The man who is employed for wages is as much a business man as his employer;
    - the attorney in a country town is as much a business man as the corporation counsel in a great metropolis;
    - the merchant at the cross-roads store is as much a business man as the merchant of New York;
    - the farmer who goes forth in the morning and toils all day, who begins in the spring and toils all summer, and who by the application of brain and muscle to the natural resources of the country creates wealth, is as much a business man as the man who goes upon the Board of Trade and bets upon the price of grain;
    - the miners who go down a thousand feet into the earth, or climb two thousand feet upon the cliffs, and bring forth from their hiding places the precious metals to be poured into the channels of trade are as much business men as the few financial magnates who, in a back room, corner the money of the world.
    - We come to speak of this broader class of business men.

Confirmation: Ah, my friends, we say not one word against those who live upon the Atlantic Coast,

- but the hardy pioneers who have braved all the dangers of the wilderness,
- who have made the desert to blossom as the rose, the pioneers away out there [pointing to the West]
- who rear their children near to Nature's heart, where they can mingle their voices with the voices of the birds—out there where they have erected schoolhouses for the education of their young, churches where they praise their Creator, and cemeteries where rest the ashes of their dead—these people,
- we say, are as deserving of the consideration of our party as any people in this country. [encomium]
- It is for these that we speak. We do not come as aggressors. Our war is not a war of conquest; we are fighting in the defense of our homes, our families, and posterity. [metaphor]
- **We** have petitioned, and our petitions have been scorned; **we** have entreated, and our entreaties have been disregarded; **we** have begged, and they have mocked when our calamity came. We beg no longer; **we** entreat no more; we petition no more. **We** defy them! [anaphora]
- The gentleman from Wisconsin [Vilas] has said that he fears a Robespierre. My friends, in this land of the free you need not fear that a tyrant will spring up from among the people [invective]. What we need is an Andrew Jackson to stand, as Jackson stood, against the encroachments of organized wealth.
- They tell us that this platform was made to catch votes.
    - We reply to them that changing conditions make new issues; that the principles upon which Democracy rests are as everlasting as the hills,
    - but that they must be applied to new conditions as they arise.
- Conditions have arisen, and we are here to meet those conditions. They tell us that the income tax ought not to be brought in here; that it is a new idea.

- They criticize us for our criticism of the Supreme Court of the United States. My friends, we have not criticized; we have simply called attention to what you already know. If you want criticisms read the dissenting opinions of the court. There you will find criticisms.
- [The law fitting. The law is just.] They say that we passed an unconstitutional law; we deny it.
  - The income tax was not unconstitutional when it was passed;
  - it was not unconstitutional when it went before the Supreme Court for the first time;
  - it did not become unconstitutional until one of the judges changed his mind,
  - and we cannot be expected to know when a judge will change his mind.
- The income tax is just. [commonplace]
  - It simply intends to put the burdens of government justly upon the backs of the people.
  - I am in favor of an income tax.
  - When I find a man who is not willing to bear his share of the burdens of the government which protects him, I find a man who is unworthy to enjoy the blessings of a government like ours.
- They say that we are opposing national bank currency; it is true. If you will read what Thomas Benton said, you will find he said that, in searching history, he could find but one parallel to Andrew Jackson [chreia];
  - that was Cicero, who destroyed the conspiracy of Cataline and saved Rome. [Tale]
  - Benton said that Cicero only did for Rome what Jackson did for us when he destroyed the bank conspiracy and saved America.
- We say in our platform we believe that the right to coin and issue money is a function of government. We believe it.
- We believe that it is a part of sovereignty, and can no more with safety be delegated to private individuals than we could afford to delegate to private individuals the power to make penal statutes or levy taxes [pathos argument: appeal to safety and security].
- Mr. Jefferson, who was once regarded as good Democratic authority, seems to have differed in opinion from the gentleman who has addressed us on the part of the minority. [Ethos]
- Those who are opposed to this proposition tell us that the issue of paper money is a function of the bank, and that the government ought to go out of the banking business.
- I stand with Jefferson rather than with them, and tell them, as he did, that the issue of money is a function of government, and that the banks ought to go out of the governing business.
- They complain about the plank which declares against life tenure in office. They have tried to strain it to mean that which it does not mean. What we oppose by that plank is the life tenure which is being built up in Washington, and which excludes from participation in official benefits the humbler members of society.
- And now, my friends, let me come to the paramount issue. If they ask us why it is that we say more on the money question than we say upon the tariff question, I reply that, if protection has slain its thousands, the gold standard has slain its tens of thousands [proverb].
- If they ask us why we do not embody in our platform all the things that we believe in, we reply that when we have restored the money of the Constitution, all other necessary reform will be possible; but that until this is done, there is no other reform that can be accomplished.

- ❑ [Tale] Why is it that within three months such a change has come over the country? Three months ago when it was confidently asserted that
  - ▪ those who believed in the gold standard would frame our platform and nominate our candidates,
  - ▪ even the advocates of the gold standard did not think that we could elect a President.
- ❑ And they had good reason for their doubt, because there is scarcely a State here today asking for the gold standard which is not in the absolute control of the Republican Party.
- ❑ But note the change. Mr. McKinley {the Republican candidate for President in that year} was nominated at St. Louis upon a platform which declared for the maintenance of the gold standard until it can be changed into bimetallism [gold and silver] by international agreement. [end of Tale]
- ❑ Mr. McKinley was the most popular man among the Republicans, and three months ago everybody in the Republican Party prophesied his election. How is it today? [Rhetorical Question]
  - ▪ Why, the man who was once pleased to think that he looked like Napoleon—that man shudders today when he remembers that he was nominated on the anniversary of the battle of Waterloo.
  - ▪ Not only that, but as he listens, he can hear with ever increasing distinctness the sound of the waves as they beat upon the lonely shores at St Helena. [analogy]
- ❑ Why this change? Ah, my friends, is not the reason for the change evident to anyone who will look at the matter? [Rhetorical Questions]
  - ▪ No private character, however pure, no personal popularity, however great, can protect from the avenging wrath of an indignant people a man who will declare that he is in favor of fastening the gold standard upon this country,
  - ▪ or who is willing to surrender the right of self-government and place the legislative control of our affairs in the hands of foreign potentates and powers. [pathos]
- ❑ We go forth confident that we shall win. Why? [Rhetorical Question]
  - ▪ Because upon the paramount issue of this campaign there is not a spot of ground upon which the enemy will dare to challenge battle. [metaphor]
  - ▪ If they tell us that the gold standard is a good thing, we shall point to their platform and tell them that their platform pledges the party to get rid of the gold standard and substitute bimetallism.
  - ▪ If the gold standard is a good thing why try to get rid of it? [Rhetorical Question]
- ❑ I call your attention to the fact that some of the very people who are in this Convention today and who tell us that we ought to declare in favor of international bimetallism—thereby declaring that the gold standard is wrong and that the principle of bimetallism is better—these very people four months ago were open and avowed advocates of the gold standard, and were then telling us that we could not legislate two metals together, even with the aid of all the world.
- ❑ If the gold standard is a good thing, we ought to declare in favor of its retention and not in favor of abandoning it; and if the gold standard is a bad thing why should we wait until other nations are willing to help us to let go? [Rhetorical Question] [Values argument]
- ❑ Here is the line of battle, and we care not upon which issue they force the fight; we are prepared to meet them on either issue or on both.

- ❏ If they tell us that the gold standard is the standard of civilization, we reply to them that this, the most enlightened of all the nations of the earth, has never declared for a gold standard and that both the great parties this year are declaring against it. If the gold standard is the standard of civilization, why, my friends, should we not have it? If they come to meet us on that issue we can present the history of our nation. [confirmation/refutation] [Logos argument]
- ❏ More than that; we can tell them that they will search the pages of history in vain to find a single instance where the common people of any land have ever declared themselves in favor of the gold standard.
- ❏ They can find where the holders of fixed investments have declared for a gold standard, but not where the masses have. Mr. Carlisle said in 1878 that this was a struggle between the "idle holders of idle capital" and "the struggling masses, who produce the wealth and pay the taxes of the country," [chreia]
- ❏ and, my friends, the question we are to decide is:
    - **Upon** which side will the Democratic party fight;
    - **upon** the side of "the idle holders of idle capital" or
    - **upon** the side of "the struggling masses"? That is the question which the party must answer first, and then it must be answered by each individual hereafter. [anaphora]
- ❏ The sympathies of the Democratic party, as shown by the platform, are on the side of the struggling masses who have ever been the foundation of the Democratic party.
- ❏ There are two ideas of government.
    - There are those who believe that if you will only legislate to make the well-to-do prosperous, their prosperity will leak through on those below.
    - The Democratic idea, however, has been that if you legislate to make the masses prosperous, their prosperity will find its way up through every class which rests upon them. [comparison]
- ❏ You come to us and tell us that the great cities are in favor of the gold standard; we reply that the great cities rest upon our broad and fertile prairies. Burn down your cities and leave our farms, and your cities will spring up again as if by magic; but destroy our farms and the grass will grow in the streets of every city in the country. [confirmation/refutation]
- ❏ My friends, we declare that this nation is able to legislate for its own people on every question, without waiting for the aid or consent of any other nation on earth; and upon that issue we expect to carry every state in the Union.
- ❏ I shall not slander the inhabitants of the fair state of Massachusetts nor the inhabitants of the state of New York by saying that, when they are confronted with the proposition, they will declare that this nation is not able to attend to its own business.
- ❏ It is the issue of 1776 over again. Our ancestors, when but three millions in number, had the courage to declare their political independence of every other nation; shall we, their descendants, when we have grown to seventy millions, declare that we are less independent than our forefathers? [chreia]

Conclusion: No, my friends, that will never be the verdict of our people.

- ❏ Therefore, we care not upon what lines the battle is fought.
- ❏ If they say bimetallism is good, but that we cannot have it until other nations help us, we reply, that instead of having a gold standard because England has, we will restore bimetallism, and then let England have bimetallism because the United States has it.

- ❑ If they dare to come out in the open field and defend the gold standard as a good thing, we will fight them to the uttermost.
- ❑ Having behind us the producing masses of this nation and the world, supported by the commercial interests, the laboring interests and the toilers everywhere, we will answer their demand for a gold standard by saying to them:
- ❑ **You shall not press down upon the brow of labor this crown of thorns, you shall not crucify mankind upon a cross of gold.**

Just in case you want to know, at the end of the speech as Bryan was saying the last line he stretched out his arms in imitation of being crucified. The audience leaped to its feet and applauded for close to seven minutes while Bryan held the cruciform in silence.

APPENDIX 1

Self-Analysis

Self-Analysis
THE FABLE EXERCISE

Name: _____ Date: _____

Title of Fable: _____

What is this fable about?

Why did you choose this fable for this audience?

What part of this exercise did you find most challenging?

Construct an argument using this fable as your evidence.

Word count: _____

Approximate Speech length in minutes/seconds: _____

Self-Analysis
THE TALE EXERCISE

Name: _____ Date: _____

Title: _____

What type of tale is this?   Check circle
- ❏ Personal Story
- ❏ Current Event
- ❏ Summary of a movie, book, play, music lyric, poem, etc.
- ❏ Other:_____

What is this story about?

Why did you choose this story for this audience?

What part of this exercise did you find most challenging?

Construct an argument using this story as evidence.

Word count: _____

Approximate Speech length in minutes/seconds: _____

Self-Analysis
CHREIA EXERCISE

Name: _____ Date: _____

Title: _____

Type of testimony (circle the chosen type)
- ❏ Expert
- ❏ Prestige
- ❏ Peer

Quote:

Counter Quote:

What does the quote mean?

What does the counter quote mean?

Why did you choose this quote for this audience?

Give an example that supports the original quote.

Construct an argument using the quote as evidence.

Word count: _____

Approximate Speech length in minutes/seconds: _____

Self-Analysis
THE PROVERB EXERCISE

Name: _____ Date: _____

Title: _____

Proverb:

Counter Proverb:

What does the proverb mean?

What does the counter proverb mean?

Give an example that supports the original proverb.

Why did you choose this proverb for this audience?

Construct an argument using the quote as evidence.

Word count: _____

Approximate Speech length in minutes/seconds: _____

Self-Analysis
THE REFUTATION EXERCISE

An exercise in highlighting the weakness of your opponent's arguments

Name: _____ Date: _____

Title: _____

Complete this sentence: I want my audience to be persuaded that _____
_____
_____

(This sentence represents your beliefs, attitudes, or values. This sentence explains what you will argue FOR.)

Circle the argument you will use to **refute** your position:

- ❏ Uncertainty
- ❏ Incredibility
- ❏ Impossibility
- ❏ Lack of Consistency
- ❏ Illogic
- ❏ Unfitting

The argument I will use to refute my position is best stated in this way: _____
_____
_____
_____
_____
_____

Why did you choose this argument?

Why do you think this argument will be effective with this audience?

Word count: _____

Approximate Speech length in minutes/seconds: _____

Self-Analysis
THE CONFIRMATION EXERCISE

An exercise in highlighting the strengths of your arguments

Name: _____ Date: _____

Title: _____

Complete this sentence: I want my audience to be persuaded that _____
_____

(This sentence represents your beliefs, attitudes, or values. This sentence explains what you will argue FOR.)

Circle the argument you will use to **support** your position:

- ❏ Uncertainty
- ❏ Incredibility
- ❏ Impossibility
- ❏ Lack of Consistency
- ❏ Illogic
- ❏ Unfitting

The argument I will use to support my position is best stated in this way:

Why did you choose this argument?

Why do you think this argument will be effective with this audience?

Word count: _____

Approximate Speech length in minutes/seconds: _____

Self-Analysis
THE COMMONPLACE EXERCISE

Name: _____ Date: _____

Title: _____

Vice to be condemned:

Virtue to be praised:

Explain how the vice has negative effects on

❏   The individual:

❏   The family:

❏   The community:

Example you will use to condemn the vice:

Choose one of these and make an argument condemning the vice:
❏   Legality
❏   Justice
❏   Possibility
❏   Honor

State the argument here:

Why did you choose this vice to condemn?

Word count: _____

Approximate Speech length in minutes/seconds: _____

Self-Analysis
THE CEREMONIAL SPEECH

Encomium

Name: _____ Date: _____

Title: _____

Who/What is the person/place/thing you choose to speak about?

Why did you choose this topic?

What virtue(s) does this person/place/thing embody that make(s) this person/place/thing praiseworthy?

What two further characteristics/deeds make this person/place/thing praiseworthy?

Why do these deeds/characteristics make this person/place/thing more praiseworthy than others?

Word count: _____

Approximate Speech length in minutes/seconds: _____

Self-Analysis
THE CEREMONIAL SPEECH

Invective

Name: _____ Date: _____

Title: _____

Who/What is the person/place/thing you choose to speak about?

Why did you choose this topic?

What vice(s) does this person/place/thing embody that make(s) this person/place/thing worthy of condemnation?

What two further characteristics/deeds make this person/place/thing worthy of condemnation?

Why do these deeds/characteristics make this person/place/thing more worthy of condemnation than others?

Word count: _____

Approximate Speech length in minutes/seconds: _____

Self-Analysis
THE INFORMATIVE SPEECH EXERCISE

Comparison

Name: _____ Date: _____

Title: _____

Complete this sentence: I want my audience to understand that

What two people/places/things/ideas are you comparing to each other?

List the three main points you will use to make your comparison.

Why did you choose these areas of comparison?

After doing this comparison what conclusion did you come to? Are the things compared equal? One better than the other? You can't decide which is equal/better?

Why did you choose this topic for this audience?

Word count: _____

Approximate Speech length in minutes/seconds: _____

Self-Analysis
THE INFORMATIVE SPEECH EXERCISE

Description

Name: _____ Date: _____

Title: _____

Complete this sentence: I want my audience to understand that

What will you describe in this speech?

List the elements you will use to describe your topic.

Why did you choose these elements?

What is the one thing you want the audience to think, believe, or do by the end of your speech?

Why did you choose this topic for this audience?

Word count: _____

Approximate Speech length in minutes/seconds: _____

Self-Analysis
THE INFORMATIVE SPEECH EXERCISE

Characterization

Name: _____ Date: _____

Title: _____

Complete this sentence: I want my audience to understand that

Who will you be portraying in this speech?

Why did you choose this person, place, or thing?

Briefly describe what you will talk about in your characterization.

Why did you choose this method of conveying information? Why do you think this is the most effective way to get your point across to your audience?

Why did you choose this topic for this audience?

Word count: _____

Approximate Speech length in minutes/seconds: _____

Self-Analysis
THE PERSUASIVE SPEECH EXERCISE

Thesis

Name: _____ Date: _____

Title: _____

Complete this sentence: I want my audience to be persuaded that

Turn the above sentence into a question.

Give a brief narrative that lays out the problem or issue you will address.

List the three arguments you will make in support of your position.

List the one or two arguments that tell against your position.

Check the box next to exercises from the Progymnasmata you will use to support and/or refute your position. Use at least three.

- ❏ Fable
- ❏ Tale
- ❏ Chreia
- ❏ Proverb
- ❏ Refutation
- ❏ Confirmation
- ❏ Commonplace

Word count: _____

Approximate Speech length in minutes/seconds: _____

Self-Analysis
THE PERSUASIVE SPEECH EXERCISE

Introduction to Law

Name: _____ Date: _____

Title: _____

Complete this sentence: I want my audience to be persuaded that _____
_____
_____

Summarize the law you wish to change.

Check the three questions you will use as your arguments for your speech:

- ❏ Was the law clearly written?
- ❏ Is the law consistent within itself?
- ❏ Is the law just?
- ❏ Is the law expedient?
- ❏ Is the law enforceable?
- ❏ Is the law practical?
- ❏ Is the law decent?

Which 2 of the questions listed above will you use to refute your position?

Check the box next to exercises from the Progymnasmata you will use to support or refute your position. Use at least three.

- ❏ Fable
- ❏ Tale
- ❏ Chreia
- ❏ Proverb
- ❏ Refutation
- ❏ Confirmation
- ❏ Commonplace

Word count: _____

Approximate Speech length in minutes/seconds: _____

APPENDIX 2

Speech Critiques

Speech Critique Sheet
FABLE

Name: _____ Date: _____

1. Of the Fables you heard today, which was presented most effectively and why?

2. Thinking of the most effective Fable, what would be a strong counter argument to the moral/point the Fable made?

3. Thinking of the most effective Fable presentation, what would you suggest to improve it? (Don't say nothing.)

4. What new information did you learn today?

5. What critique did you hear today that you will use to improve your next presentation?

Speech Critique Sheet
TALE

Name: _____ Date: _____

1. Of the tales you heard today, which was presented most effectively and why?

2. Thinking of the most effective tale, what would be a strong counter argument to the moral/point of the tale?

3. Thinking of the most effective tale presentation, what would you suggest as a way to improve it? (Don't say nothing.)

4. What new information did you learn today?

5. What critique did you hear today that you will use to improve your next presentation?

Speech Critique Sheet
CHREIA

Name: _____ Date: _____

1. Of the Chreias you heard today, which was presented most effectively and why?

2. Thinking of the most effective Chreia, explain how the counter quote or example did/did not present a strong argument against the position affirmed in the first quote.

3. How might you use this Chreia in a persuasive/thesis speech? Give a specific Speech Purpose possibility and then how this Chreia would support the position asserted.

4. What new information did you learn today?

5. What critique did you hear today that you will use to improve your next presentation?

Speech Critique Sheet
PROVERBS

Name: _____ Date: _____

1. Of the Proverbs you heard today, which was presented most effectively and why?

2. Thinking of the most effective Proverb, explain how the counter proverb, quote, or example did/did not present a strong argument against the position affirmed in the first Proverb.

3. How might you use this Proverb in a persuasive/thesis speech? Give a topic possibility and then how this Proverb would support the position asserted.

4. What new information did you learn today?

5. What critique did you hear today that you will use to improve your next presentation?

Speech Critique Sheet
REFUTATION

Name: _____ Date: _____

1. Of the Refutation speeches you heard today, which was presented most effectively and why?

2. Thinking of the most effective Refutation speech, explain why you think it was or was not a sufficient/legitimate argument against the speaker's position.

3. Suggest one other argument against the speaker's position.

4. What new information did you learn today?

5. What critique did you hear today that you will use to improve your next presentation?

Speech Critique Sheet
CONFIRMATION

Name: _____ Date: _____

1. Of the Confirmation speeches you heard today, which was presented most effectively and why?

2. Thinking of the most effective Confirmation speech, explain why you think the argument(s) presented are sufficient/legitimate argument(s) for the speaker's position.

3. Suggest one other argument for the speaker's position.

4. What new information did you learn today?

5. What critique did you hear today that you will use to improve your next presentation?

Speech Critique Sheet
COMMONPLACE

Name: _____ Date: _____

1. Of the Commonplace speeches you heard today, which was presented most effectively and why?

2. Thinking of the most effective Commonplace, explain why it was or was not a sufficient/legitimate argument against the vice the speaker condemned.

3. Suggest one other argument/example that supports the speaker's position.

4. What new information did you learn today?

5. What critique did you hear today that you will use to improve your next presentation?

# Speech Critique Sheet
ENCOMIUM

Name: _____ Date: _____

1. Of the Encomium speeches you heard today, which was presented most effectively and why?

2. Thinking of the most effective Encomium speech, explain why the speech sufficiently explained why this person/place/thing is worthy of praise.

3. What information about the person/place/thing was most persuasive to you? Why?

4. What new information did you learn today?

5. What critique did you hear today that you will use to improve your next presentation?

Speech Critique Sheet
INVECTIVE

Name: _____ Date: _____

1. Of the Invective speeches you heard today, which was presented most effectively and why?

2. Thinking of the most effective Invective speech, explain why you think the speech sufficiently explained why this person/place/thing is worthy of censure.

3. What information about the person/place/thing was most persuasive to you? Why?

4. What new information did you learn today?

5. What critique did you hear today that you will use to improve your next presentation?

Speech Critique Sheet
COMPARISON

Name: _____ Date: _____

1. Of the Comparison speeches you heard today, which was presented most effectively and why?

2. Thinking of the most effective Comparison speech, what was it about the comparison that made this a good speech? Organization? Main point? Language choice?

3. What information contained in the Comparison was most persuasive to you? Why? (If this is a double encomium are you convinced the two things compared are equal? If this is an encomium/invective are you convinced that one thing is worse than the other?)

4. What new information did you learn today?

5. What critique did you hear today that you will use to improve your next presentation?

Speech Critique Sheet
CHARACTERIZATION

Name: _____ Date: _____

1. Of the Characterization speeches you heard today, which was presented most effectively and why?

2. Thinking of the most effective Characterization speech, explain how the central idea was successfully argued.

3. What information about the person characterized in the speech was new to you?

4. Explain why/why not the use of characterization is a good rhetorical strategy.

5. What critique did you hear today that you will use to improve your next presentation?

Speech Critique Sheet
THESIS

Name: _____ Date: _____

1. Of the Thesis speeches you heard today, which was presented most effectively and why?

2. Thinking of the most effective Thesis speech, explain why you consider the speaker persuasive.

3. What was the speaker's strongest argument in favor of the position asserted?

4. What was the speaker's weakest argument?

5. What, in your opinion, is the strongest argument against the speaker's position?

6. What new information did you learn today?

7. What critique did you hear today that you will use to improve your next presentation?

Speech Critique Sheet
INTRODUCTION TO LAW

Name: _____ Date: _____

1. Of the Introduction to Law speeches you heard today, which was presented most effectively and why?

2. Thinking of the most effective Introduction to Law speech, explain why the speech sufficiently argued for its position.

3. Which argument was the least effective?

4. Which argument was the most effective?

5. What new thing did you learn today?

6. What critique did you hear today that you will use to improve your next presentation?

BIBLIOGRAPHY

Ad Herenium, [Cicero], Ad G. Herennium: De ratione dicendi (Rhetorica ad Hernnium). trans. Harry Caplan. (Loeb Classical Library, 1954).

Aristotle (1955). *The Ethics of Aristotle: The Nichomachaen Ethics.* (rev. ed.) (J. K. Thomson, trans.). New York: Viking. p. 104.

Ballef, Michelle, and Michael G. Moran. *Classical Rhetorics and Rhetoricians: Critical Studies and Sources.* Westport, CT: Praeger Press, 2005.

"Brainy Quotes." Accessed March 16, 2014. http://www.brainyquote.com/quotes/r.html.

Chowdhury, Rohini. "longlongtimeago.com." Last modified 4/2010. Accessed March 27, 2014. http://www.longlongtimeago.com/llta_fairytales_snow_white.html.

"Chreia." *Anordoll's Blog* (blog), 9/24/2011. http://anordall.wordpress.com/2011/09/24/chreia/ (accessed March 11, 2014).

Conan Doyle, Arthur. Authorama, "The Adventure of the Bruce-Partington Plans." Last modified 4/2003. Accessed March 6, 2014. http://www.authorama.com/adventure-of-the-bruce-partington-plans-1.html.

Copi, Irving M. and Cohen, Carl. *Introduction to Logic.* Prentice Hall, 1998.

Corbett, Edward P. J. *Classical Rhetoric for the Modern Student.* New York: Oxford University Press, 1965.

Crowley, Sharon and Hawhee Debra, *Ancient Rhetorics for Contemporary Students. 3rd ed.*, New York: Pearson Longman, 2004.

Doing Rhetorical History: Concepts and Cases. ed. Kathleen J. Turner. Tuscaloosa: University of Alabama Press, 1998.

Hanson, Victor Davis. *Carnage and Culture: Landmark Battles in the Rise of Western Culture.* New York: Random House, Inc. 2001.

Hurley, Patrick J. *A Concise Introduction to Logic.* Thornson Learning, 2000.

"Illustrated World of Proverbs." Accessed March 18, 2014. http://www.worldofproverbs.com

Institutio oratoria. (Quintilian) Trans. H. E. Butler. (Loeb Classical Library, 1920–22).

Internet Movie Data Base (IMDB), "Synopsis for Snow White and the Huntsman 2012." Last modified 02/2013. Accessed March 18, 2014. http://www.imdb.com/title/tt1735898/synopsis?ref_=ttpl_pl_syn.

Invectives, (Petrarca) Trans. by David Marsh. (Harvard Univ. Press, 2003)

Investopedia USA, Accessed April 2, 2014. investopedia.com.

Jerome, Richard, and Bob Meadows. *People* Magazine, "Saving Lives." Last modified Oct. 02, 2006. Accessed March 11, 2014. http://www.people.com/people/archive/article/0,,20060609,00.html.

Kennedy, George A., *A New History of Classical Rhetoric*. Princeton: Princeton University Press, 1994.

Kopan, Tal. Politico, "10 things to know: Arizona SB 1062." Accessed April 1, 2014. http://www.politico.com/story/2014/02/arizona-sb1062-facts-104031.html?hp=l8).

Merriam-Webster. An Encyclopedia Britannica Company, Accessed April 2, 2014. merriam-webster.com

MSN News, "People Who Famously Blew Their Money." Accessed March 31, 2014. http://news.msn.com/pop-culture/people-who-famously-blew-their-money

Murphy, James J., *A Short History of Writing Instruction: From Ancient Greece to Modern America*, 2nd ed. Mawah, NJ: Lawrence Erlbaum, 2001.

National Constitution Center, "ConstitutionCenter.org." Accessed March 17, 2014. http://constitutioncenter.org/constitution/the-amendments/

Official Proceedings of the Democratic National Convention Held in Chicago, Illinois, July 7, 8, 9, 10, and 11, 1896 (Logansport, Indiana, 1896).

Pitts, Breana. "Bleacherreport." Accessed March 27, 2014. http://bleacherreport.com/articles/1175781-4-reasons-kobe-bryant-is-still-better-than-lebron-james.

"Proverbs Around the World." Accessed March 19, 2014. http://www.memorablequotations.com/proverb.html.

Sellnow, Deanna D., *Public Speaking: A Process Approach*. New York: Harcourt College Publishers, 2002.

The Art of Rhetoric (Aristotle) Trans., John Henry Freese (Loeb Classic Library, 1982).

Turner Classic Movies, "Snow White and the Seven Dwarfs" (1937). Accessed March 27, 2014. http://www.tcm.com/tcmdb/title/90631/Snow-White-and-the-Seven-Dwarfs/.

University of Minnesota, "University of Minnesota Human Rights Library." Last modified 3/11/2014. Accessed March 19, 2014. http://www.umn.edu/humanrts/education/all_amendments

University of North Carolina Chapel Hill, "The Writing Center." Accessed March 14, 2014. http://writingcenter.unc.edu/handouts/fallacies/.

University of Southern California, "Proverbs Resource." Accessed March 19, 2014. http://cogweb.ucla.edu/Discourse/Proverbs/Miscellaneous.html.

CPSIA information can be obtained
at www.ICGtesting.com
Printed in the USA
FSHW020235111219
64952FS